Umbrella in the Storm

How to Successfully Weather Life

Barbara Shoner

Novel Idea Press

Umbrella in the Storm: How to Successfully Weather Life
Copyright © 2018 by Barbara Shoner

All rights reserved. No portion of this book may be reproduced, stored in a retrieval system, or transmitted in any form or by any means—electronic, mechanical, photocopy, recording, or any other—except for brief quotations in printed reviews, without the prior written permission of the publisher.

Unless otherwise indicated, all Scripture quotations are taken from the Holy Bible, New Living Translation, copyright © 1996, 2004, 2015 by Tyndale House Foundation. Used by permission of Tyndale House Publishers, Inc., Carol Stream, Illinois 60188. All rights reserved. Scripture quotations marked (NIV) are taken from the Holy Bible, New International Version®, NIV®. Copyright © 1973, 1978, 1984, 2011 by Biblica, Inc.™ Used by permission of Zondervan. All rights reserved worldwide. www.zondervan.com. The "NIV" and "New International Version" are trademarks registered in the United States Patent and Trademark Office by Biblica, Inc. ™ Scripture quotations marked NKJV are taken from the New King James Version®. Copyright © 1982 by Thomas Nelson. Used by permission. All rights reserved. Scripture quotations marked MSG are taken from THE MESSAGE, Copyright © 1993, 1994, 1995, 1996, 2000, 2001, 2002, 2003 by Eugene H. Peterson. Used by permission of NavPress Publishing Group. All rights reserved. Represented by Tyndale House Publishers, Inc. Scripture quotations marked ERV are taken from the HOLY BIBLE: EASY-TO-READ VERSION © 2001 by World Bible Translation Center, Inc. and used by permission. Scriptures marked as "(CEV)" are taken from the *Contemporary English Version* Copyright © 1991, 1992, 1995 by American Bible Society, Used by Permission. Scripture quotations marked NASB are taken from the *New American Standard Bible*, Copyright © 1960, 1962, 1963, 1968, 1971, 1972, 1973, 1975, 1977, 1995 by The Lockman Foundation. Used by permission.

ISBN-13: 978-0-9799081-1-8
Printed in the United States of America
Published by Novel Idea Press
For more information or to order add'l copies visit www.barbarashoner.com

DEDICATION

This book is dedicated first and foremost to the Lord Jesus Christ, because I am nothing apart from Him. I'd never make it through the storms of life without grabbing tightly (with both fists clenched, knuckles white, fingers numb) onto my Umbrella. I pray to never let go.

To Samantha, Kaci and Jacob, the three angels I've been blessed with who are truly the best children in the world (sorry everyone, but it's true). As you start on your own journeys down the path of life, I'm so thankful each one of you carries your Umbrella. I pray you never let go.

To my mom, thank you for being there for me through the adventures of my sometimes cloudy but mostly sunny life.

To my readers, may you always find the rainbow.

CONTENTS

DEDICATION		iii
INTRODUCTION		1
1.	UNEXPECTED STORMS When Trials Rain Down	3
2.	DOPPLER RADAR Storms are on the Way	15
3.	BATTEN DOWN THE HATCHES Preparing Ourselves Spiritually	23
4.	CYCLONES Destruction of Unforgiveness	35
5.	TSUNAMIS Overcoming Waves of Grief	47
6.	TORNADOES Green Skies of Jealousy & Envy	59
7.	OVERCAST Effects of Illness	71
8.	WILDFIRES The Heat of Anger	83
9.	TROPICAL DEPRESSION Finding Joy	93
10.	INNER AND OUTER RAINBANDS Suffering the Effects of Ourselves and Others	103
11.	STORM SHELTER His Protection Even Through God-Sent Storms	115

12.	RIDING THE STORM OUT	125
	Drawing Closer to God	
13.	TRAVEL ALERT	137
	Storms Don't Mean You're Out of God's Will	
14.	IN THE EYE OF THE STORM	147
	Be Still and Wait on God	
15.	BLIZZARDS	157
	Time to Shovel the Driveway (Move!)	
16.	SEA OF STORMS	167
	Anchored in Faith	
17.	FLOOD OF GRACE	177
	God's Grace Washes Over You	
18.	DANCING IN THE RAIN	185
	The Power of Praise	
19.	RAINBOWS	193
	Promises of God	

Invitation: Accepting the Free Gift of the Umbrella	201
Discussion Questions	203
Photos	211
Review	217
About the Author	218
References	220

INTRODUCTION

Life is full of storms. Some are annoying sprinkles, while others become full-blown catastrophes. Just as an umbrella can shield you from the spattering of rain, when the storms of life pour down—sickness, death, divorce, addiction, debt, abuse, betrayal, loss of a job, shattered dreams, broken hearts—Jesus can be your protection if you determine to hold onto Him. The Umbrella of Christ will not flip inside out or fly away in severe storms. It withstands even hurricane-force winds.

This book navigates the treacherous waters of life's challenges, and offers biblical and practical insights to ride out these storms. Instead of mooring our boats to be battered against the dock, let's release all that is tying us down and set sail for calm waters, anchoring our hope in Jesus.

"The name of the Lord is a fortified tower; the righteous run to it and are safe" (Proverbs 18:10).

CHAPTER 1

UNEXPECTED STORMS
When Trials Rain Down

When you go through deep waters, I will be with you. When you go through rivers of difficulty, you will not drown. When you walk through the fire of oppression, you will not be burned up; the flames will not consume you (Isaiah 43:2).

Often there are telltale signs a storm is brewing. Clouds darken, the wind gusts, the temperature drops and there's a damp smell in the air.

Sometimes life's storms can be forecasted. Your husband or wife starts coming home from work a little later; your boss won't look you in the eye; your child starts acting belligerent; the lump is not going down.

There are many times, though, when storms hit without any warning. As quick as a lightning bolt, tragedy can strike.

Living in Florida, I often witness unexpected nature storms. Beachgoers frolic until a sudden downpour has them frantically grabbing their gear and scurrying for cover. There are times when it even rains while the sun is shining! It was during such a time of favorable conditions when I found myself caught in the fury of a storm I never saw coming.

On my knees in the stark, sterile hospital bathroom I sobbed. I almost welcomed the cold, hard tile bruising my shins—the pain a reality check in an unreal day. Surely this had to be a nightmare. But the crackly voice over the loudspeaker presented another harsh reminder that down the hall my two-day-old baby girl lay under a surgeon's scalpel.

In my human weakness I wanted to scream at God, "Why? Why is this happening?" Instead I pleaded, "God help us!"

Just three days earlier my life sparkled like the sun glistening on calm waters. An ecstatic first-time pregnant mom, I eagerly awaited the arrival of my baby. During my pregnancy I did everything I could to ensure a healthy child. I ate wholesome foods and played classical music to my unborn baby through headphones stretched across my belly. I even taped myself reading Bible stories and *Goodnight Moon* to play to her.

Too early to detect anything, my only ultrasound at thirteen weeks turned out to be a blessing. I continued through my pregnancy blissfully imagining what my baby would look like and dreaming of the person he or she would be.

The crashing waves of reality would pound us soon enough.

One early evening in October, through clenched teeth I informed the nurse I had to push. After checking to see how far I had dilated, she looked up with fear in her eyes.

"Hold on! Don't push!" The nurse rushed out of the room in search of the doctor.

My husband and I locked eyes. We both noticed a change in the atmosphere. The doctor charged in and after a quick examination shouted orders to the nurses. The overwhelming urge to push surpassed my ability to comprehend anything else and the pain engrossed my fear.

The welcoming cry of my baby soon greeted me, but after cleaning her up and placing a cap on her head, the nurse gave us only a quick glimpse of Samantha before rushing her to ICU. The frenzy of hospital room activity left us unaware of the severity of the storm. The doctor was reluctant to answer the main question swirling around: "What's wrong with my baby?" Choosing to wait for the specialists, the doctor only told us there was a problem with Samantha's head.

The nurses tended to their normal routine of settling me into a room but I was not about to rest. I hadn't even counted Samantha's fingers and toes. With hospital gown flapping and my shell-shocked husband and a trail of fussing nurses behind me, I raced down the hallway to ICU where my daughter lay in a square box-like crib.

Finally conceding to my pleas, we were given special gowns and instructed to sanitize before meeting our baby. At first sight, wires crisscrossed everywhere. My seven pound baby girl looked so tiny and terrified. Never in all of my daydreams did I envision this.

Every ounce of my being longed to hold her. I anxiously sat down in a rocking chair and a nurse gently placed Samantha in my arms. I inspected body parts and caressed what skin I could touch between the wires. A perfect little body—until I took off her hat.

A large bulging mass protruded from the top of her head. It was horrifying, and yet nothing had ever looked more beautiful to me than this little bundle of flesh God created through my husband and me.

Samantha remained in ICU that night with the Lord gently rocking her in His arms while I laid awake in my bed mentally holding her. I begged for the specialist to see me as soon as possible and thankfully she came to my bedside at 6:30 a.m. Finally we would learn the extent of the damage. However, the storm proved to be even more destructive than our first assessment.

"Your daughter was born with a rare disorder called encephalocele," the doctor said with reluctance. "It's a neural tube defect."

Her neural tube didn't close completely while she was being formed, causing a mound of brain matter and membranes to protrude through an opening in her skull. Because it involved the brain the doctor couldn't tell us what our baby's abilities would be, except to say there is usually intellectual and developmental disabilities along with a myriad of other problems.

We would have to wait and see.

An intensive five-hour brain surgery to put the part of her brain outside of the skull back into place and close the opening loomed on the horizon, scheduled to hit the following day. But for now Samantha was allowed to stay with me and I cherished every single moment. Free from the wires, she acted just like any other baby and with her little cap on I could almost forget anything was wrong.

That is, until I couldn't nurse her for eight hours prior to surgery. Not being able to explain to my newborn baby why I was ignoring her piercing shrieks for food for hours on end ranks as one of the most horrifying experiences in my life.

When her cries had quieted from the anesthetic and she was wheeled into surgery, I cried out to the Lord on that cold tile floor. Suddenly, a peace came over me with the comforting realization that while I had known my daughter for only a few days, the Lord knew her before she was even formed. She was God's workmanship and He loved her with perfect and everlasting love. The Lord protects His children, and a determination rose in me to stand strong, be positive, and fight for my baby too.

After the surgery when I sat in a hospital chair holding my precious girl for four long days, I continually felt the inexplicable peace of God reassuring me everything was going to be okay. Just as I clung tightly to my baby, I knew God would never let go of us.

Two weeks later I found myself back in that same bathroom. During her after-surgery checkup the doctor discovered Samantha also had hydrocephalus, or "water on the brain." This brain condition occurs when the fluid cushioning the brain and spinal cord gets trapped and is unable to drain from the brain. This next surgery involved the neurosurgeon placing a shunt into a ventricle space in Samantha's brain and running tubing into her abdomen to drain and regulate the excess fluid. This would keep the spinal fluid from building up and putting pressure on her brain. Samantha would have this valve her entire life.

One thing she wouldn't have is part of her brain.

The neurosurgeon pointed to a place on the scan where a section of Samantha's brain was missing, but the doctor couldn't say what the absent part controlled. What she could say was Samantha would definitely be physically and mentally challenged and to "just love her for who she is." That became the doctor's catch phrase, but they were not the words any parent ever expects to hear.

We had been hit by a storm of catastrophic proportions.

I believe many of us can attest to going through seasons in our lives when we are enjoying a mountaintop experience only to then feel the earth shift below us, unexpectedly thrusting us into an avalanche of despair. We struggle to find a foothold—anything to stop the descent—and as we are buried, we wonder how we could have gotten caught in such a situation.

Whether your storm is a slight drizzle or a deadly force, all trials cause discomfort on some level. Often we are left with the aftermath of wondering how and why such a thing occurred. Believers might even question why they were ever in the storm's path when they clearly felt they were following Jesus.

Yet the Bible tells us God "lets the sun rise for all people, whether they are good or bad. He sends rain to those who do right and to those who do wrong" (Matthew 5:45 ERV). No one is exempt from the struggles of life. Even those closest to Jesus were caught in unexpected storms:

> As evening came, Jesus said to his disciples, "Let's cross to the other side of the lake." So they took Jesus in the boat and started out, leaving the crowds behind (although other boats followed). But soon a fierce storm came up. High waves were breaking into the boat, and it began to fill with water.
>
> Jesus was sleeping at the back of the boat with his head on a cushion. The disciples woke him up, shouting, "Teacher, don't you care that we're going to drown?"
>
> When Jesus woke up, he rebuked the wind and said to the waves, "Silence! Be still!" Suddenly the wind stopped, and there was a great calm. Then he

asked them, "Why are you afraid? Do you still have no faith?"

The disciples were absolutely terrified. "Who is this man?" they asked each other. "Even the wind and waves obey him!" (Mark 4:35-41)

Even though the disciples were experienced fishermen, the intensity of this storm caused them to panic and to seriously question whether the Lord cared for them. Often our first defense in a life storm is to panic. We may even doubt the Lord's love for us, especially when He doesn't seem to be paying any attention to our problems. Like the disciples, we fear He is "sleeping on the job," or worse yet, He simply doesn't care.

Just because we are surprised by unexpected storms, though, the Lord isn't. He knows exactly what's going to happen, and He is right there with us whether we realize it or not.

Jesus will calm our storms, but first He wants us to trust Him. While it's natural to be afraid in trying times, the Lord wants us to have faith and not fear. The disciples didn't need to be frightened. Jesus already told them they were going to "cross to the other side of the lake." While it wasn't smooth sailing, Jesus' protection was over them and in His perfect timing He stopped the storm.

Although sometimes we may go through trials longer than we like, God uses these times to strengthen our character. The disciples didn't cry out to Jesus until *after* the boat began filling with water. Often we don't remember to rely on Jesus until we are at the end of ourselves either. Big storms remind us how small and powerless we are—and how giant and powerful our God is.

In the Book of Acts, a religious extremist named Saul encountered a big storm and an even bigger God. Zealous and dedicated to his mission, Saul knew his exact purpose. Or so he thought.

Traveling down the road to Damascus on a ruthless quest to destroy Christians, Saul uttered threats as he walked with determination, confident in his calling to serve God by persecuting the church.

Until an unexpected storm knocked him off his feet:

> As he neared Damascus on his journey, suddenly a light from heaven flashed around him. He fell to the ground and heard a voice say to him, "Saul, Saul, why do you persecute me?"
>
> "Who are you, Lord?" Saul asked.
>
> "I am Jesus, whom you are persecuting," he replied. "Now get up and go into the city, and you will be told what you must do."
>
> The men traveling with Saul stood there speechless; they heard the sound but did not see anyone. Saul got up from the ground, but when he opened his eyes he could see nothing. So they led him by the hand into Damascus. For three days he was blind, and did not eat or drink anything. (Acts 9:3-9 NIV)

The storm blinded him. For three days Saul suffered in darkness, deprived of food, humbled and dying to himself until the Lord confirmed Saul to be alive in Christ and would follow His plan instead.

Many of us have also faced unexpected, life-altering experiences. Some of us have even traveled our own road to Damascus. In Paul's instance, his hardship ultimately changed his life for the better. The Lord humbled Paul but didn't leave him broken. Paul became passionately in love with Christ and the Lord used him in mighty ways. Interestingly, God said this about Paul: "I will show him how much he must suffer for my name" (Acts 9:16 NIV). As close as Paul became to the Lord, he still experienced adversity.

The Old Testament tells of a man named Job who suffered unforeseen catastrophic storms. Job was a righteous man, serving the Lord and minding his own business. In fact, the Lord said of Job: "There is no one on earth like him; he is blameless and upright, a man who fears God and shuns evil" (Job 1:8 NIV). Yet in one day Job was hit by not one but *four* devastating storms. All of his livestock and servants were either killed or carried away by thieves and every one of his ten children died. On top of that he was inflicted with excruciating sores!

Storms of this magnitude are incomprehensible and many well-meaning people try to save God's reputation by blaming all bad weather on satan. However, the story of Job proves otherwise. After patrolling the earth one day, satan appeared before the Lord and during their conversation God commended righteous Job. Satan accused God of giving Job special favor and he wagered Job would stop serving God if the Lord discontinued blessing him.

"All right, you may test him," the Lord *said to Satan. "Do whatever you want with everything he possesses, but don't harm him physically"* (Job 1:12 emphasis added).

Satan left and proceeded to take away Job's children, livestock, and servants—all of his earthly possessions. Yet Job did not sin by blaming God. Satan once again appeared before the Lord.

> Then the Lord asked Satan, "Have you noticed my servant Job? He is the finest man in all the earth. He is blameless—a man of complete integrity. He fears God and stays away from evil. And he has maintained his integrity, even though you urged me to harm him without cause."

> Satan replied to the Lord, "Skin for skin! A man will give up everything he has to save his life. But reach out and take away his health, and he will surely curse you to your face!"
>
> *"All right, do with him as you please," the Lord said to Satan. "But spare his life."* So Satan left the Lord's presence, and he struck Job with terrible boils from head to foot. (Job 2:3-7 emphasis added)

As demonstrated in the Book of Job, satan only has the power to do what the Lord allows. God is in control!

There is no comfort in denying God's sovereignty by portraying Him as only loving. Such a view disrespects God and limits what He can do in our lives. He is All-Powerful, All-Knowing, All-Loving, and Never-Changing.

I find more assurance in serving an Almighty God who can fix anything if He chooses, rather than relying on a God who can't change something even if He wanted to.

Nothing is impossible with God! In His omniscience, He will either turn your situation around or use your circumstances to change you. Even though you may not understand when storms strike, be assured God is in the winds of adversity. And just like with Job, God tells satan he can only go so far. The Lord promises: "Surely, as I have planned, so it will be, and as I have purposed, so it will happen" (Isaiah 14:24 NIV). Keep trusting, keep believing, and keep persevering. Jesus' light shines brighter than the noonday sun and will pierce through any fog.

Peace comes with the understanding that even though you can't control the weather, you can hold onto the Umbrella for protection. The same power the Lord used to stop the wind will calm your seas.

Unexpected Storms

PRAYER

"Yours, O Lord, is the greatness, the power, the glory, the victory, and the majesty. Everything in the heavens and on earth is yours, O Lord, and this is your kingdom. We adore you as the one who is over all things. Wealth and honor come from you alone, for you rule over everything. Power and might are in your hand, and at your discretion people are made great and given strength."[1] I ask You, Lord, to give me the strength and grace I need to endure unexpected storms. Don't allow the waves of adversity to crush me against the rocks, but lead me instead to calm waters. Thank You, Lord, for using these trials to transform me just as pounding surfs reshape landscapes. I will trust in You and You will be glorified. In the name of Jesus, My Deliverer, I pray, Amen!

CHAPTER 2

DOPPLER RADAR
Storms are on the Way

Here on earth you will have many trials and sorrows. But take heart, because I have overcome the world (John 16:33).

There is a rhyme that is used to forecast the weather: *Red sky at night, sailor's delight. Red sky at morning, sailors take warning.*

Jesus even knew of this expression and He commented on it in Matthew 16:2-3: "When evening comes, you say, 'It will be fair weather, for the sky is red,' and in the morning, 'Today it will be stormy, for the sky is red and overcast.' You know how to interpret the appearance of the sky, but you cannot interpret the signs of the times" (NIV).

Evidently, there is truth to this saying. The scientific basis comes from the fact that red skies indicate the clouds are filled with moisture and dust. The direction storms move in is generally from west to east. Since the sun sets in the west, a red sunset would mean the sun is illuminating departing clouds from a low pressure system (storms) and there is now high pressure air, which means stable conditions and good weather.

On the other hand, when the sun rises in the east (the same direction storms move to), a red sunrise means the sun is shining on approaching clouds which are filled with moisture, indicating heavy rain could be on its way.

There are other unusual methods to predict weather without the use of technology: a circle around the moon indicates rain or snow is coming soon; higher clouds mean fairer weather, whereas low hanging clouds mean rain; flowers are more fragrant just before it rains; curly, frizzy hair means higher humidity; and some people say their joints hurt before a storm.

Life storms can be predicted in the Bible. Many Scriptures point to the inevitable reality of challenges in life:

"My brethren, count it all joy **when** you fall into various trials" (James 1:2 NKJV).

"Yes, and all who desire to live godly in Christ Jesus **will** suffer persecution" (2 Timothy 3:12 NKJV).

"Life is short and sorrowful for **every** living soul" (Job 14:1 CEV).

"I [Jesus] have told you these things, so that in me you may have peace. In this world you **will** have trouble. But take heart! I have overcome the world" (John 16:33 NIV).

"You **will** be hated by everyone because of me, but the one who stands firm to the end will be saved" (Matthew 10:22 NIV).

Notice these verses express the words "will" and "when," not "if." Numerous other Scriptures in the Bible also confirm we are destined to encounter bad weather. We live in a fallen, sinful world and there's an enemy who desires to destroy us. Satan wants to ruin your health, your marriage, your children, your finances, and your faith. He's been plotting against you before you were even born and will continue to wage war against you throughout your days. He doesn't want you to draw closer to the Lord, minister to others, or walk in your destiny. His purpose is to steal, kill, and destroy. He wants to devour you with lies, insecurities, doubts, fears, discouragement, busyness…anything to take your focus off God. He brings storms of adversity right when you are on the verge of something good. He wants you to give up before your breakthrough.

Don't quit! These storms were already in the forecast. 1 Peter 4:12-14 points out: "Dear friends, don't be surprised at the fiery trials you are going through, as if something strange were happening to you. Instead, be very glad—for these trials make you partners with Christ in his suffering, so that you will have the wonderful joy of seeing his glory when it is revealed to all the world."

Refuse to allow fear to consume you. Remember, even though satan took one-third of the angels with him when he was tossed out of heaven, two-thirds still serve God. Satan is already outnumbered and fallen angels are no match for the Lord! While we do need to prepare for bad weather, 1 John 4:4 declares: "He [God] who is in you is greater than he [satan] who is in the world" (NKJV). Rest assured, satan is limited by the Lord in what he can do because even he is under the authority of God.

Doppler radar picked up storm activities from the time of the fall of Adam and Eve, God's first created beings. After being placed in a perfect setting in the Garden of Eden with one rule from God not to eat from the tree of the knowledge of good and evil, satan slithered in and deceived them. Choosing to listen to the devil instead of God, Adam and Eve ate the forbidden fruit, causing sin and death to enter the world. Immediately their eyes were opened to their sins and they attempted to hide in shame from the Lord.

We went from a perfect world to a broken one cursed by sin. Storm activity brewed from that point forward, and—although these are necessary actions for our growth as Christians—no amount of reading our Bible, going to church, paying our tithes, praying, and being compassionate towards others will stop the formation of storms.

Thankfully, God, who is rich in mercy, walked in the garden to seek after them. Even though He knew Adam and Eve had sinned, the Lord still protected them. Their storm left them naked with only fig leaves as covering. The fig leaves would soon wither, but God graciously took care of His precious children. "The Lord God used animal skins and made some clothes for the man and his wife. Then he put the clothes on them" (Genesis 3:21 ERV).

The Lord does the same for us today. He seeks after us even when we are too embarrassed to be found. When we mess up, He wraps us in His grace. When we fall for the lies of the enemy, the Lord will meet us right where we are and our shame will be covered by the righteousness of Jesus when we confess and repent.

Not only are we under a weather advisory from spiritual attacks, but all types of storms that rage in life. Jesus warns us that if we are to be devoted disciples, we must endure these storms. In Luke 9:22 Jesus said, "It is necessary that the Son of Man proceed to an ordeal of suffering, be tried and found guilty by the religious leaders, high priests, and religion scholars, be killed, and on the third day be raised up alive."

Then Jesus explained what we as true followers can expect:
> If any of you want to be my followers, you must give up your own way, take up your cross daily, and follow me. If you try to hang on to your life, you will lose it. But if you give up your life for my sake, you

will save it. And what do you benefit if you gain the whole world but are yourself lost or destroyed? (9:23-25)

The Message Bible describes it in part this way: "Anyone who intends to come with me has to let me lead. You're not in the driver's seat—I am. Don't run from suffering, embrace it. Follow me and I'll show you how."

This assures us that as believers we don't have to worry about the storms that will rage in our lives when we let Jesus lead the way. We can rest in the peace described in the Psalms: "You lead me to streams of peaceful water, and you refresh my life. You are true to your name, and you lead me along the right paths. I may walk through valleys as dark as death, but I won't be afraid. You are with me" (Psalms 2-4).

The Lord continually refreshed my life following the birth of my daughter, and His presence held me together. After spending the first few weeks of Samantha's life in and out of the hospital, I was finally able to focus solely on my baby. Even though Doppler radar still indicated storm activity, life's demands took my eyes off the clouds and onto the tasks at hand. I had a newborn whose entry into the world proved traumatic and she greatly needed to be cared for. She knew nothing about future milestones she might not meet. She simply wanted to be fed, changed, snuggled and loved.

I settled into my role like other mothers: feeling sleep deprived; hoping to take a shower once in a while; eating while holding my baby; and wearing "eau de puke" as my perfume. I also melted each time she gazed at me; laughed at every coo; thought the sun rose from her smiles; and felt a contentment beyond explanation whenever I watched my baby's lips puckering in tune with her deep breaths of sleep.

When adversity strikes we can't hunker down and hide. Life still has to be lived. Meals need to be prepared, the house cleaned, diapers changed, bills paid. Once storms hit we can't reverse the damage—we can only rebuild the future.

I could have fretted and read into every movement of my child. Anxiety could've ruled my days and haunted my nights. But a negative atmosphere can create a fearful child and a myriad of other issues. In the midst of storms, positive attitudes are the raincoats we need to wear.

My daughter's future forecast indicated more challenges than the average person and she needed me to encourage and believe in her. I, in turn, had to trust God to keep me optimistic and to give us both strength. While I couldn't change any medical diagnosis, I could point out the sunshine and teach my child to look for the rainbows.

Being caught in a downpour is no one's idea of a pleasant time, but rain is necessary. Where there's no rain, there's desert. To escape the barrenness and enjoy lushness, we must put up with rainfall. Storms help us grow. They cause us to turn our faces upward and search for the Light. Our roots dig deeper and we seek the shelter of the Lord Most High. Because of the rain we can bear fruit.

Pastor Harry Emerson Fosdick described it this way: "He who knows no hardships will know no hardihood. He who faces no calamity will need no courage. Mysterious though it is, the characteristics in human nature which we love best grow in a soil with a strong mixture of troubles."

The storms of life will continue to rage until Jesus returns to restore His Kingdom. The Bible says, "You will soon hear about wars and threats of wars, but don't be afraid. These things will have to happen first, but that isn't the end. Nations and kingdoms will go to war against each other. People will starve to death, and in some places there will be earthquakes. But this is just the beginning of troubles" (Matthew 24:46-48 CEV).

There will come a time, however, when with the clouds will come the Son. For believers, His glory will shine like the brightness of lightning and no more will we be battered by the storms. We are promised: "He will wipe all tears from their eyes, and there will be no more death, suffering, crying, or pain" (Revelation 21:4 CEV). Hallelujah!

PRAYER

Oh Lord, what a glorious God You are! Even though storms are guaranteed to come, disaster is not imminent. Help me to keep my eyes on You through all trials. I ask for Your protection against the storms of satan. When I forget and want to hide in fear, please remind me that You are ultimately in control and even satan is under Your authority. In all storms of life, whatever the source, I thank You that I am not alone. You are always with me. I pray these storms will help me to boldly take up my cross and be a true follower of Christ. I pray for Your peace to always quiet my soul no matter what the Doppler radar shows. I pray this in the name of Jesus, My Protector, Amen!

CHAPTER 3

BATTEN DOWN THE HATCHES
Preparing Ourselves Spiritually

You can go to God Most High to hide. You can go to God All-Powerful for protection. I say to the Lord, *"You are my place of safety, my fortress. My God, I trust in you." God will save you from hidden dangers and from deadly diseases. You can go to him for protection. He will cover you like a bird spreading its wings over its babies. You can trust him to surround and protect you like a shield* (Psalm 91:1-4 ERV).

The expression "batten down the hatches" is a nautical term used to express how a crew prepares the ship when heading into rough seas. The hatches (doors) are closed and secured shut with batten (strips of wood or other material).

The Merriam-Webster's Collegiate Dictionary also gives this definition: "To prepare for a difficult or dangerous situation." Since the Bible warns us life storms are inevitable, we should always be prepared.

No matter where you live, some form of natural disaster is possible. Whether it is hurricanes, earthquakes, tornadoes, tsunamis, snowstorms, lightning, heat waves, wildfires, or mudslides, your area most likely offers vital safety information and a disaster preparedness checklist to help you prepare in the event of a natural disaster. Although we store away canned goods, water, first aid kits, candles, batteries, flashlights, and plan our evacuation route, many of us are completely unprepared for a life storm.

God's Word warns us to be ready at all times. Matthew 25:1-13 tells a parable about ten virgins who were on their way to meet the bridegroom. Five in the group were wise and the other five were foolish. While the wise ones brought extra oil for their lamps, the foolish ones brought none. When the bridegroom's arrival was delayed, the girls grew tired and fell asleep.

At midnight they were awakened by a voice informing them the bridegroom had arrived and it was time to meet him. The wise virgins tended to their lamps, adding more oil in preparation for the meeting. However, because they came unprepared, the foolish virgins had no oil to refill their flickering lamps so they raced off to purchase the needed oil. In the meantime, the prepared virgins went into the banquet room with the bridegroom and the door closed behind them.

When the others returned they banged on the door and begged to be admitted, but the bridegroom denied their entry. They had missed their opportunity.

God's Word advises us to be prepared, and similar to planning for a natural disaster, we should keep ourselves ready. Just as we stock our cupboards and board up our windows, our spirits should be full and our minds sealed off from the enemy who is waiting to attack us.

Batten Down the Hatches

In Florida we prepare for hurricanes, and one of the most important items on the checklist is water. Our spiritual checklist must also include water: the "Living Water" of Christ. Just as you would not be able to survive a natural disaster for long without water, your eternal life depends on living water.

In the Gospel of John when Jesus spoke to a Samaritan woman, He told her, "Anyone who drinks this water will soon become thirsty again. But those who drink the water I give will never be thirsty again. It becomes a fresh, bubbling spring within them, giving them eternal life" (4:13).

Jesus explained about "living water" again in 7:37-39:
> "Whoever is thirsty may come to me and drink. If anyone believes in me, rivers of living water will flow out from their heart. That is what the Scriptures say." Jesus was talking about the Spirit. The Spirit had not yet been given to people, because Jesus had not yet been raised to glory. But later, those who believed in Jesus would receive the Spirit. (ERV)

Those who feel an insatiable thirst may try to quench it with alcohol, drugs, work, relationships, money—but they will soon become thirsty again. Only the Living Water of Christ can satisfy a thirsty soul.

When you draw closer to the Lord and His teachings, the Holy Spirit will be a fresh bubbling spring within you, guiding and directing you. Allow it to flow freely in your life and onto the lives of those around you. The Lord promises: "To all who are thirsty I will give freely from the springs of the water of life. All who are victorious will inherit all these blessings, and I will be their God, and they will be my children" (Revelation 21:6-7).

Another item on our storm readiness checklist is food. As food is necessary to keep our bodies alive, Jesus is essential for our spiritual life. In John 6:35 Jesus said, "I am the bread that gives life. No one who comes to me will ever be hungry. No one who believes in me will ever be thirsty" (ERV).

He also said, "I am the living bread that came down from heaven. Whoever eats this bread will live forever. This bread is my body. I will give my body so that the people in the world can have life" (John 6:51 ERV).

We fill our emergency supply with canned goods, and we also need to stock up on the Bread of Life in order to survive the storms. We must nourish our souls with Jesus, filling it through prayer, praise, worship, and the Word.

The Bible describes a time when Jesus was in a wilderness place. Taken there to be tempted by the devil, Jesus didn't eat for forty days and forty nights. Afterwards, the devil approached Jesus during a time of weakness and hunger (watch out, he still uses that same trick on us). The devil tempted Jesus, saying: "If you are the Son of God, tell these stones to become loaves of bread."

But Jesus told him, 'No! The Scriptures say, "People do not live by bread alone, but by every word that comes from the mouth of God"' (Matthew 4:3-4).

Jesus overcame through the power of Scripture, and the Word of God should also be our first defense in the face of a storm. No squall from the devil is a match for the tempest of God. "Submit yourselves, then, to God. Resist the devil, and he will flee from you" (James 4:7 NIV).

Also on the list of emergency supplies are candles, flashlights, and batteries. We require light to penetrate the darkness and the light of Jesus is bright enough for any storm. Jesus said, "I am the

Light of the World. Whoever follows me will never walk in darkness, but will have the light of life" (John 8:12 NIV).

In a world where we are surrounded by darkness, Jesus declares if we follow Him then He will light our way. Like plants that grow toward the sun and bugs that are drawn to light, we too should be drawn to His light.

Not only will Jesus pierce the darkness of our storms, He then charges us to be lights for Him. The Bible tells us:

> You are the light that shines for the world to see. You are like a city built on a hill that cannot be hidden. People don't hide a lamp under a bowl. They put it on a lampstand. Then the light shines for everyone in the house. In the same way, you should be a light for other people. Live so that they will see the good things you do and praise your Father in heaven. (Matthew 5:14-16 ERV)

Jesus is our battery, the power source that causes His light to shine through us and illuminate the way for others. As the moon only reflects the light of the sun, we too are to be reflectors of the Son. Together we will be ready for any storm when we can boldly profess: "The LORD is my light and my salvation—so why should I be afraid?" (Psalm 27:1).

Before a storm arrives, it is important to have adequate shelter. A safe place that can withstand the pounding of damaging winds. Our walls must be sturdy with prayer and fortified by the Word of God. Jesus revealed:

> Everyone then who hears these words of mine and does them will be like a wise man who built his house on the rock. And the rain fell, and the floods came, and the winds blew and beat on that house,

but it did not fall, because it had been founded on the rock. And everyone who hears these words of mine and does not do them will be like a foolish man who built his house on the sand. And the rain fell, and the floods came, and the winds blew and beat against that house, and it fell, and great was the fall of it. (Matthew 7:24-27 ESV, emphasis added)

When your life is built on the strong foundation of Jesus, He will shelter you from the storms. He will keep you safe and you will then be strong enough to withstand any pressure from the elements.

"The LORD is my rock, my fortress, and my savior; my God is my rock, in whom I find protection. He is my shield, the power that saves me, and my place of safety" (Psalm 18:2).

Another key survival tactic is to know your evacuation plan. Understanding the way out of impending disasters is important, and you should also be aware of your spiritual escape plan. Preparing ahead of time spiritually will minimize the effects of a storm. A life-changing moment can happen at any time. The key is to be prepared.

Our evacuation plan is in the Bible and it gives us clear direction on how to get prepared for the storms of life the Lord warns us *will* come. "Keep alert at all times. And pray that you might be strong enough to escape these coming horrors and stand before the Son of Man" (Luke 21:36).

Noah prepared for the storm. He didn't wait until he saw dark clouds gathering or felt raindrops falling. While others surely laughed at him for spending many, many years building an ark when no one had ever even experienced rain, by faith Noah continued to build. He prepared ahead of time, remaining faithful and following the Lord's instructions. He then had what he needed for him and his family to survive the most deadly of storms.

Be proactive and get ahead of the storm. Begin fulfilling your checklist by first being sure you've accepted Christ as your Savior and are filled with the living water of the Holy Spirit. Your shelves should be stocked with the Word of God and your heart and mouth overflowing with praise and thanksgiving. Build a closer relationship with the Lord by establishing a prayer life and by trusting and allowing God to be Lord over your life. Accept His will to be sovereign, and above all, remember He loves you with an everlasting love.

Even though the news following my daughter's birth knocked me down, it didn't take me out because I had some preparation. From the moment I knew a life was forming inside me I continually laid my hands on my belly and prayed for my unborn child. I spoke words of affirmation over my baby and asked the Lord to empower me to be the best mom possible. I trusted God's sovereignty over the life of my child and when the storm hit I experienced a measure of peace and strength beyond my own capability because I had already been stockpiling God's Word.

The Lord also provides another way for us to batten down the hatches. Ephesians 6:10-18 tells us we can prepare by putting on the full armor of God. We have an enemy who is ready to launch any type of attack to destroy us and the Lord does not leave us unprotected:

> Be strong in the Lord and in His mighty power. Put on all of God's armor so you will be able to stand firm against all strategies of the devil. For we are not fighting against flesh-and-blood enemies, but against evil rulers and authorities of the unseen

world, against mighty powers in this dark world, and against evil spirits in the heavenly places. Therefore, put on every piece of God's armor so you will be able to resist the enemy in the time of evil. Then after the battle you will still be standing firm.

The devil is no match against Almighty God, and Scripture says when we dress in all of God's armor we will be able to stand strong. However, we must choose to "put on" God's armor. It's a purposeful decision. The Lord gives us the resources, but it's up to us to determine to use them.

Also, the Bible says the protection is there when we use "every piece" of God's armor. We don't pick and choose which pieces of armor to embrace and which to discard. You wouldn't board up the windows of your home against an impending storm but leave the front door wide open. Using all of the armor ensures no area is exposed.

The armor of God allows us to "stand firm." This means we will not retreat. We will hold our ground and not give up any of God's territory. Through God's power we will stand strong and be victorious!

The big storms will come when we are most vulnerable: tired, feeling under the weather, troubles at work, cranky kids, shaky relationships. But the full armor of God strengthens us to stand firm in our faith and not retreat into falling for the lies of the enemy or going back to any areas of darkness. As believers we are in the Light, sealed with the Spirit, and we can hold that position through Christ!

The first piece of God's armor is the "belt of truth." God's truth encircling us like a belt will hold us together through the storms.

Surrounded by His truth, we ought to start by being truthful about ourselves and ask the Lord as David did: "Search me, O God, and know my heart; test me and know my anxious thoughts. Point out anything in me that offends you" (Psalm 139:23-24).

Embrace God's truth in your heart and be familiar enough with His Word to recognize when the enemy is whispering lies to you, because satan will definitely try to deceive you. He will occupy your mind with taunting thoughts: you're not good enough; no one cares about you; you'll never amount to anything; you have to have this car, that house, someone's else's spouse to be happy; God doesn't love you; God can't use you; do it anyway because no one will ever find out.... The lies will swirl around you like a funnel cloud until you are completely caught up in them unless you are securely fastened to God's truth. The solid foundation is the truth of God's Word and He says you are valuable, you are chosen, you are loved, you have purpose, and you will prevail!

We are given the second piece of armor, the "breastplate of righteousness," through Christ our Savior by His death, resurrection, and gift of salvation to us. When we put on this "breastplate" our hearts are protected.

The Bible says, "Above all else, guard your heart, for everything you do flows from it" (Proverbs 4:23). Be careful though, because the enemy's arrows can penetrate this spiritual breastplate if we allow chinks to develop in the armor through our own disobedience, unforgiveness, pride, unbelief, or other unconfessed sins.

Jesus' righteousness conquers the enemy. We "put on" His righteousness when we seek the Lord above all else and allow Him to guide our lives; when we study His Word and practice godly choices; and when we live in love and become more like Christ.

The next piece of armor we are to be fitted with are "shoes of the gospel of peace." The Lord wants us to dig in our heels and stand our ground, but also be committed to moving in whatever direction He leads and to readily share the gospel with others. Just as shoes protect our feet, the Good News protects our souls, and we should be eager and willing to share that peace. First Peter 3:15 states: "Always be prepared to give an answer to everyone who asks you to give the reason for the hope that you have" (NIV).

The fourth piece of armor is the "shield of faith" and it's our first barrier of protection and used to stop the arrows of the enemy. "But without faith no one can please God. We must believe God is real and He rewards everyone who searches for him" (Hebrews 1:6 CEV).

It is through faith that the walls of Jericho fell down. By faith the people walked through the Red Sea on dry land; and because of her faith, Rahab was saved. "Faith makes us sure of what we hope for and gives us proof of what we cannot see" (Hebrews 11:1 CEV).

When we have faith in God's Word, satan's arrows fall short. We'll believe in God's everlasting love for us instead of the "God doesn't care" lies of the devil. We will trust we are redeemed through Christ and we won't fall for the accusations of the enemy. We'll know we are overcomers instead of overpowered. The arrows of doubt, fear, depression, guilt, and discouragement won't pierce us. "For every child of God defeats this evil world, and we achieve this victory through our faith" (1 John 5:4).

A helmet is worn to shield the head, and as our next piece of armor, the hope we have in our salvation and the coming Kingdom safeguards our minds. This "helmet of salvation" puts a different perspective on the storms we get caught in when we realize this is not our home, and through Christ's gift of salvation we have the promise of a rainbow beyond the thunderclouds.

Jesus' sacrifice on the cross protects our thoughts against the despair of this world and encourages us with the knowledge that our sins are forgiven when we confess them and repent, and we will spend eternity with the Lord. When we are assured of our salvation, we can have a peace that surpasses all understanding no matter what happens to us.

The helmet of salvation guards our minds against worldly thoughts:

> The weapons we use are not human ones. Our weapons have power from God and can destroy the enemy's strong places. We destroy people's arguments, and we tear down every proud idea that raises itself against the knowledge of God. We also capture every thought and make it give up and obey Christ. (2 Corinthians 10:4-5 ERV)

When we put on the helmet of salvation and become equipped with the wisdom of God through the power of the Holy Spirit, we'll learn to be more careful with our thoughts as we gain the mind of Christ. Romans 12:2 advises: "Don't change yourselves to be like the people of this world, but let God change you inside with a new way of thinking. Then you will be able to understand and accept what God wants for you. You will be able to know what is good and pleasing to him and what is perfect" (ERV).

The final piece of armor, the "sword of the Spirit," is the Word of God. This powerful weapon can be used to both fend off an attack and also deliver blows to the enemy.

Jesus used the Word of God to defeat satan when He was tempted in the desert. Three times Jesus quoted Scripture when He was under attack, and the devil then left Him. The Word of God from our mouths will do the same. When satan tells us the storms are too strong, we have the power of God's Word to slash through his lies. When we are confronted, the sword of the Spirit gives us answers to fight back with.

Hebrews 4:12 explains: "For the word of God is living and powerful, and sharper than any two-edged sword, piercing even to the division of soul and spirit, and of joints and marrow, and is a discerner of the thoughts and intents of the heart."

The sword of the Spirit has the power to change and transform lives. We can speak the Word of God over our situations. Whenever disaster threatens to overtake us, we have the promises of Scripture to cling to. There is power in the Word of God!

Storms loom on the horizon. Let's stock up on the Word of God and fill ourselves with the Holy Spirit so we can batten down the hatches and endure whatever life challenges come our way.

PRAYER

God All-Powerful, You are my mighty shield. With You I can batten down the hatches and ride out any storm, knowing You will keep me safe. As I put on the full armor of God in preparation for the battles to come, please help me to be a faithful soldier and stand strong for Christ. Lead me to victory! Help me to stay on the task of stocking my spiritual cupboards and filling my Holy Spirit generator. My eyes are on You, Lord, and in You I take refuge. No storm is too strong for All-Mighty God! Jesus, thank You for being my firm foundation. I pray this in the name of Jesus, Bread of Life, Amen!

CHAPTER 4

CYCLONES
Destruction of Unforgiveness

When you are praying and you remember that you are angry with another person about something, forgive that person. Forgive them so that your Father in heaven will also forgive your sins (Mark 11:25 ERV).

Unforgiveness can be as damaging as a cyclone, ripping apart lives in its path. Thoughts of the boss who fired you, the person who lied or stole from you or the lover who broke your heart can tear you up inside, causing collateral damage to anything in your vicinity. Even though they may be at fault, Jesus tells us we are to forgive. If we don't forgive, God doesn't forgive us.

"If you forgive those who sin against you, your heavenly Father will forgive you. But if you refuse to forgive others, your Father will not forgive your sins" (Matthew 6:14-15). To receive forgiveness we must extend forgiveness. And who of us hasn't needed to be forgiven at some point?

My mother remarried when I was eight. It turned out the man she selected to be my stepfather suffered from mental illness. He often experienced jealous fits of rage and beat my mother to the point where I'd have to run to the neighbor's house for help, always in fear of him chasing after me.

He'd throw away my dance trophies and other personal items, then punish my mom when she'd sneak them back out of the trash. He found it funny to hide under my bed, then reach out and grab my legs when I walked near it. He'd tap on my window in the middle of the night until I tiptoed over to investigate the source of the sound. As my tiny face smooshed against the glass and fearful eyes strained to see through the dark, out of nowhere he'd shove his face against the screen and growl. I'm not sure whose scream was louder!

On the nights my mom was brave enough to lock him out, my little brother and I would stand in the hallway away from windows, holding onto each other while he broke the glass to get in. Thankfully, a few years later he disappeared from our lives forever—and out of my mind too, or so I thought. Survival mode kicked in and I determined to forget.

However, even through my 20's a particular dream haunted me. I'd continually wake up in the middle of the night, drenched with sweat. In my dream, I was always running through neighborhoods trying to find a place to hide from someone chasing after me. As I frantically darted from house to house I never found a safe haven and would wake up shaking.

I finally grew tired of running, and realized this must be more than an ordinary nightmare. During my prayer time it became clear to me that my stepdad still stalked me. I hadn't forgotten after all. I just ran.

Cyclones

I felt the Lord urging me to forgive. But why? He had stolen my innocence, my childhood. The only thing he ever taught me was how to fear. Even as an adult I struggled to trust. My life was forever altered by the things my stepfather had done. Yet to stop the dreams, to quit running and to feel real joy in my life, I had to forgive.

Forgiving is a choice, not a feeling. If we forgave only when we felt like it, we'd never forgive. Also, every act of forgiveness isn't instantaneous. There may be occasions when you make up your mind to travel down the road to forgiveness, but find it still takes your heart a little longer to catch up. Sometimes it's a process. But every step closer to total forgiveness is a step towards a deeper relationship with the Lord.

When I resolved to forgive I gave the Lord permission to work in my spirit, and over time I released every bit of resentment. The nightmares stopped.

Years later when I started working with a homeless ministry, I met many people dealing with mental health issues similar to my stepfather's problems. As I befriended them, the Lord filled me with compassion instead of fear or resentment.

Forgiving is not the same as forgetting. We may not always completely forget certain circumstances, but they don't hold the same pain and they become a learning tool. Instead of resenting that I might have been a different person without those traumatic experiences, I choose to believe I am exactly the person God wants me to be in spite of them—or even because of them.

The Bible tells the story of a young man named Joseph who, at the age of seventeen, experienced a life-changing storm. His father's favorite, a lot spoiled and maybe a little arrogant, Joseph's brothers deeply resented him. One day when his brothers were out working, Joseph brought them their lunch and ended up at the bottom of a well. The brothers intended for him to die there until a caravan of slave traders happened to pass by. With money in their pockets, they waved good riddance to Joseph as he was taken to Egypt and sold into slavery.

Joseph spent many years as a slave, then he was imprisoned after being betrayed by yet another. Finally, Joseph was released and became second in command after correctly interpreting the Pharaoh's dream. The dream revealed that seven years of famine were on the way, and being forewarned, Joseph stored up grain during the plentiful years. Because of this, the Lord used Joseph to save the people from starvation.

Joseph's brothers and father lived in Canaan and when they ran out of grain, the brothers traveled to Egypt to buy more. Joseph now looked and dressed like an Egyptian and the brothers didn't recognize him—but Joseph knew them. Seeing his brothers after all that time must have been like tearing the scab off a wound. Joseph didn't immediately forgive, but after testing them to see if their hearts were now right, Joseph revealed to his brothers who he was.

> Joseph could stand it no longer. There were many people in the room, and he said to his attendants, "Out, all of you!" So he was alone with his brothers when he told them who he was. Then he broke down and wept. He wept so loudly the Egyptians could hear him, and word of it quickly carried to Pharaoh's palace.
>
> "I am Joseph!" he said to his brothers. "Is my father still alive?" But his brothers were speechless! They were stunned to realize that Joseph was

standing there in front of them. "Please, come closer," he said to them. So they came closer. And he said again, "I am Joseph, your brother, whom you sold into slavery in Egypt. But don't be upset, and don't be angry with yourselves for selling me to this place. It was God who sent me here ahead of you to preserve your lives. This famine that has ravaged the land for two years will last five more years, and there will be neither plowing nor harvesting. God has sent me ahead of you to keep you and your families alive and to preserve many survivors. So it was God who sent me here, not you! And he is the one who made me an adviser to Pharaoh—the manager of his entire palace and the governor of all Egypt." (Genesis 45:3-8)

Joseph not only forgave his brothers, he saved them. He elected to forget what might have been and instead focused on what was. He extended mercy and wisely explained: "You intended to harm me, but God intended it all for good. He brought me to this position so I could save the lives of many people" (Genesis 50:20).

Sometimes God allows the storms of betrayal to fulfill His purpose. This might not seem fair, but He's God and we're not. He sees into the future and we don't.

Forgiveness is vital not only for spiritual reasons, but also for our own health. Anger, bitterness, hatred, and vengefulness eat away at our core, making us physically sick. Every part of our being, from our bodies to our enjoyment of life, can be affected. Often, while unforgiveness is stealing our joy, the people who have wronged us aren't even thinking twice about it. Their actions are still controlling us.

The thought that the other person is "getting away with it" is one reason people find it so hard to forgive. He or she was the one in the wrong and it's not fair. But most of the time people who have wronged us don't believe they were wrong anyway. Trying to keep them locked up in our jail of unforgiveness only throws away the key to our happiness. We become the prisoner instead. While they are moving forward with their lives, we are chained to our past.

Forgiving doesn't make the other person right, it just frees us from the bondage of unforgiveness. Romans 12:19 tells us: "Do not take revenge, my friends, but leave room for God's wrath, for it is written: 'It is mine to avenge; I will repay,' says the Lord" (NIV).

It is difficult not to exchange evil for evil. You may have fantasized about getting even with the other person and spent countless hours plotting theatrically-worthy revenge. But the Lord says the final curtain call is His, even if you were an innocent stagehand.

David had every reason to avenge himself against Saul. The King relentlessly hunted David to kill him, even though David had done nothing wrong. One night while Saul and his army sought David, Saul went into a cave and fell asleep. David crept in and stood before the king, unnoticed. David had the opportunity to kill his enemy right then, but he didn't. Instead he said, "As surely as the LORD lives, *the* LORD *himself will punish Saul*" (1 Samuel 26:10 ERV, emphasis added).

Forgiving sometimes takes letting go of a victim mentality and the need to be right. Don't stay stuck in the past, but take responsibility for where you are at this moment. Be careful not to use "victim talk," and instead speak in a more empowering way. Rather than seeing yourself as a victim, celebrate being a survivor!

Forgiveness doesn't mean we are denying what happened or condoning their actions. Rather, we are being obedient to God through our act of forgiving. The Lord tells us to "show mercy to others. Be kind, humble, gentle, and patient. Don't be angry with each other, but forgive each other. If you feel someone has wronged you, forgive them. Forgive others because the Lord forgave you" (Colossians 3:12-13 ERV).

Forgiving someone doesn't always mean the relationship will be healed or that the other person will change. Only the Lord can change someone. But the act of forgiving changes *us* and offers a peace otherwise lost.

The family of a victim in the mass shooting that took place at the Pulse nightclub in Orlando chose peace when they decided to forgive the shooter: "We forgive the shooter. We talked about it," said Deonka's father, a pastor who runs a nonprofit that helps the poor and elderly. "Hatred will find a way to destroy you, so we forgive the shooter. It wasn't very hard to do. Anger was in me and there was no place to release it. Forgiveness was the way to release it."[1]

Corrie ten Boom, a concentration camp survivor, said, "Forgiveness is the key that unlocks the door of resentment and the handcuffs of hatred. It is a power that breaks the chains of bitterness and the shackles of selfishness."[2]

She certainly understood the power of forgiveness. Corrie is one of the most inspirational people when it comes to forgiving. In her book, *The Hiding Place*, Corrie described how she survived prison, a concentration camp, and a death camp after being caught during WWII hiding Jews from the Germans. She suffered horrible atrocities at the hands of SS guards. Many years after her release, Corrie was brought face to face with one of the guards while on tour to share her experiences. The guard had the nerve to extend his hand and ask for her forgiveness. Visions of the excruciating pain this man had caused threatened to overtake her. Still, through the grace and strength of the Lord she decided to forgive.

Corrie wrote, "When He tells us to love our enemies, He gives, along with the command, the love itself."[2]

The Bible tells of a man named Stephen who chose to extend that same mercy. His simple act of sharing the gospel caused him to be dragged out of the city and stoned to death. Yet, "[w]hile they were stoning him, Stephen prayed, 'Lord Jesus, receive my spirit.' Then he fell on his knees and cried out, 'Lord, do not hold this sin against them.' When he had said this, he fell asleep" (Acts 7:59-60 NIV). What an inspiring act of forgiveness empowered by God!

The act of forgiving will be different depending on the circumstances, and will be revealed through the wisdom of Christ. Sometimes you may be called to forgive the other person face to face or through correspondence. The best approach at times may be to write a letter to release all of your feelings, but never actually send the letter. Sometimes, like in my circumstance, the other person isn't around any longer and the only person you can share your forgiveness with is God. Sometimes forgiving needs to only take place with the Lord.

Forgiveness may call for self-examination to check whether we are contributing in any way to the situation or if we are judging too harshly. It's sometimes easier to see the errors of others than our own. In a discussion about forgiveness, the Apostle Peter asked Jesus, "Master, how many times do I forgive a brother or sister who hurts me? Seven?" Jesus told him not seven times but seventy times seven, then He related this story:

> "So God's kingdom is like a king who decided to collect the money his servants owed him. The king began to collect his money. One servant owed

him several thousand pounds of silver. He was not able to pay the money to his master, the king. So the master ordered that he and everything he owned be sold, even his wife and children. The money would be used to pay the king what the servant owed.

"But the servant fell on his knees and begged, 'Be patient with me. I will pay you everything I owe.' The master felt sorry for him. So he told the servant he did not have to pay. He let him go free. (Matthew 18:23-27 ERV)

Later, the servant who had been forgiven confronted a person who owed *him* money and demanded immediate payment. Even though the man begged him to be patient and promised to repay everything he owed, the servant refused and had the man thrown in jail.

When the master found out, he said, "You evil servant. You begged me to forgive your debt, and I said you did not have to pay anything! So you should have given that other man who serves with you the same mercy I gave you" (18:32-33). Then he directed the servant to be thrown in jail.

At the end of the parable, Jesus informed, "This king did the same as my heavenly Father will do to you. You must forgive your brother or sister with all your heart, or my heavenly Father will not forgive you" (18:35). Unfortunately, many people are happy to be forgiven but they don't want to forgive. However, Jesus commands us to forgive over and over again.

Sometimes the person we may need to forgive is ourselves. Many of us find it easier to forgive others than ourselves. We beat ourselves up over things that can't be undone anyway. We say things about ourselves that would completely horrify us if someone else were to say them to us. We replay events over and over in our minds, rehearsing new lines while pounding ourselves with the old ones. We dwell on regrets and start believing every lie the enemy feeds us.

I had to learn to forgive myself when my daughter was born with a birth defect. Did I do something to cause it? I was thirty when I found out we were expecting and I thought I did everything I could to ensure a healthy child. My cravings consisted of grapefruit, strawberries and tomatoes—healthy choices I believed. But did I eat too much acidic foods? When I heard not having enough folic acid can contribute to structural birth defects, I beat myself up for not taking vitamins before getting pregnant.

I later learned that while the exact cause of an encephalocele is not known, it is believed to be a mixture of genetics and environmental factors and not due to anything a mother did or did not do during pregnancy. Even though the condition was caused by factors outside of my control, I allowed the devil to taunt me for a season.

Maybe you've messed up. We all do to some degree at times in our lives. Take that wrong choice to the Lord in prayer and ask Him for forgiveness. Confess any sins and then move on. The Lord already has. His Word says if you confess your sins He is faithful to forgive your sins, and He then "remove[s] our sins as far from us as the east is from the west" (Psalm 103:12). He also promises: "I will forgive their wickedness, and I will never again remember their sins" (Hebrews 8:12).

Unforgiveness towards yourself will bring self-destruction, but forgiving will bring peace and restoration.

Negative thinking steals our focus away from being the person God would have us to be. One of the most effective ways I have found to retrain my thinking is to follow the advice of Philippians 4:8, which says to fix our thoughts on "what is true, and honorable, and right, and pure, and lovely, and admirable. Think about things that are excellent and worthy of praise.…Then the God of peace will be with you."

When you find your mind wandering down a dark alley, bring it into the light by purposefully thinking positive thoughts. Singing praise songs and praying out loud really helps. It's very difficult to sing and think bad thoughts at the same time. It takes practice, but you *can* take every dark thought captive. You cannot change what already happened, so stop watching reruns and move forward into a new season.

You may be sifting through the rubble in the aftermath of a self-made storm, but burying yourself in it won't help you rebuild. Pull yourself out by God's extended hand of grace. Start restructuring your being to fit the blueprints of the Lord's plan for your life.

Whether our cyclone of unforgiveness is aimed toward others or ourselves, the greatest example of forgiveness comes from Jesus Himself when He was crucified. His accusers had whipped Him mercilessly and then led him to a cross:

> Two others, both criminals, were led out to be executed with him. When they came to a place called The Skull, they nailed him to the cross. And the criminals were also crucified—one on his right and one on his left.
>
> Jesus said, "Father, forgive them, for they don't know what they are doing." (Luke 23:32-34 NIV).

Through Jesus' selfless act of sacrifice we have all been forgiven, and it is through His power we can also learn to forgive and live as the Lord commands in Ephesians 4:32: "Be kind and loving to each other. Forgive each other the same as God forgave you through Christ" (ERV).

PRAYER

Lord, You are the King of forgiveness. Thank You for removing my sins as far as the east is from the west. Help me to forget them just as You have. Cover my mind with the blood of Jesus and no longer allow instant replays of past mistakes to overtake my mind. And as You have forgiven me, please help me to forgive others. It doesn't matter what they have done because their past wrongs are between You and them. All that matters is my being right with You by forgiving them as You command. Help me to not only forgive, but to also have peace in my heart and soul. Lord, I likewise pray for those I've wronged to forgive me. Please give me the courage to ask for their forgiveness when appropriate. Thank You, Jesus, for Your grace and gift of forgiveness. In the name of Jesus, My Restorer, I pray, Amen!

CHAPTER 5

TSUNAMIS
Overcoming Waves of Grief

Weeping may last through the night, but joy comes with the morning (Psalm 30:5).

Waves of grief can crash ashore in different strengths—death of a loved one, loss of a relationship, sickness, broken promises, lost opportunities, betrayal—but they all have the power to knock us down. Sometimes we'll receive a storm warning, but at other times our back will be to the waves and we'll unexpectedly be thrown to the ground.

Merriam-Webster defines the word *grief* as "a deep and poignant distress; an unfortunate outcome." Whether your grief is over the death of a loved one or is another form of distress, we will all share some type of grief in this life.

While knowing a tsunami will inevitably strike at some time won't completely prepare you, realizing you will not be alone in your grief can be comforting. The Lord will be with you through it, and there will be people who have also experienced grief and can lend support. The Bible says, "God is our merciful Father and the source of all comfort. He comforts us in all our troubles so that we can comfort others. When they are troubled, we will be able to give them the same comfort God has given us" (2 Corinthians 1:3-4).

God doesn't intend for you to weather the storms on your own. We are called to help one another. There's an African proverb that says, "If you want to go fast, go alone. If you want to go far, go together."

Life is a marathon, so we need one another. Don't be afraid to turn to others for support because there will come a time when you will also be used in the same way. In your time of need, accept help from other people because they can hold you up in times of weakness, remind you of God's goodness when all you regard at the moment is bad, and encourage you in your faith. Then, when you are ready, God will use you to bless the lives of others in similar circumstances—which may even distract you from your own grief.

When you are surrounded by darkness and the waves threaten to drag you under, it is important to understand that mourning does not mean a lack of faith. David was a man after God's own heart, yet he grieved terribly when his son, Absalom died:

> The king was overcome with emotion. He went up to the room over the gateway and burst into tears. And as he went, he cried, "O my son Absalom! My son, my son Absalom! If only I had died instead of you! O Absalom, my son, my son." (2 Samuel 18:33)

It is okay to grieve. Jesus cried many times. Hebrews 5:7 relates: "While Jesus was here on earth, he offered prayers and pleadings, with a loud cry and tears, to the one who could rescue him from death. And God heard his prayers because of his deep reverence for God."

Jesus wept over the death of his friend, Lazarus, even though He knew He would be bringing Lazarus back to life. He wept for the pain of Lazarus' loved ones. John 11:33-35 says:

> When Jesus saw her weeping, and the Jews who had come along with her also weeping, he was deeply moved in spirit and troubled.
>
> "Where have you laid him?" he asked.
>
> "Come and see, Lord," they replied.
>
> *Jesus wept.* (emphasis added)

The shortest, most moving statement in the Bible: "Jesus wept." Since Jesus Himself cried, He certainly doesn't expect us not to. Many believers are under the false assumption that a strong Christian is not to display any vulnerable emotions during a time of crisis because doing otherwise would be demonstrating a lack of faith.

However, Jesus shows us it's natural to experience times of sadness. Allow yourself to go through the grieving process in whatever manner you need: some people withdraw, while some find comfort in reaching out to others; some exhibit devastation, while others act numb as they go about "business as usual." There is no "right way" to grieve, but it's important to remember we do not grieve like others who have no hope. The Bible promises us:

> My friends, we want you to understand how it will be for those followers who have already died. *Then you won't grieve over them and be like people who don't have any hope.* We believe that Jesus died and was raised to life. We also believe that when God brings Jesus back again, he will bring with him all who had faith in Jesus before they died. With a loud command and with the shout of the chief angel and

a blast of God's trumpet, the Lord will return from heaven. Then those who had faith in Christ before they died will be raised to life. Next, all of us who are still alive will be taken up into the clouds together with them to meet the Lord in the sky. *From that time on we will all be with the Lord forever.* Encourage each other with these words. (1 Thessalonians 4:13-18 CEV, emphasis added)

In terms of the death of loved ones who are believers, even though we miss having them here with us, we have the hope of being reunited with them again. For those who die in a cloud of uncertainty as to whether they were believers, we don't know what last minute opportunity they were given and how they responded. God's Word declares: "The Lord is not slow about His promise, as some count slowness, but is patient toward you, *not wishing for any to perish but for all to come to repentance*" (2 Peter 3:9 NASB, emphasis added). Turn to the Lord for peace, and use that uncertainty to fuel a determination to share the saving grace of Jesus with as many people as possible.

While I've suffered the grief of losing loved ones, I have also experienced grief in other forms. I've grieved the loss of a marriage—a tsunami that hit me from behind and knocked me down for a while. By the grace of God, though, I was able to unbury myself from the sand, shake it off, and find the peace to move forward. It was a process that involved great dependence on the Lord, much prayer and worship, help from others who understood what I was going through, and a time of mourning and forgiving. It meant turning to Jesus as Husband, knowing only He can love with an everlasting love, and trusting that He will always be there during the lonely hours. It took being hopeful that my tomorrows would be better than my heartbreaking yesterdays, and believing He really would restore beauty from the ashes.

When my first daughter was born, I grieved over my baby being the statistical one of three percent born with a birth defect. That storm came without warning and it clouded the cheery anticipation of first-time motherhood. Fear rolled in. Since only time would tell the extent of damage to her brain from the encephalocele and hydrocephalus, the giant red scar down the back of her bald head and the outline of the valve bulging from above her right ear served as a constant reminder of the uncertainty. I grieved the loss of my expectations as I tied frilly bonnets over her head to shield us from the stares and questions of others.

However, through the sheer joys of motherhood—the sunny smile of my baby when she stared at my face with eyes full of love, her tiny hand clenched tightly to my finger; the sweet scent of her skin; the pure magic of her giggles—and with the ever-present comfort of the Lord, I turned my pain into praise.

The Book of Psalms is filled with glorious praises to the Lord, but many of them started with pain that then led to praise. In Psalm 61, David begins by crying out to the Lord: "Please listen, God, and answer my prayer! I feel hopeless, and I cry out to you." David then does a 180, completely changing his attitude to finish the Psalm with: "I will sing your praises forever and will always keep my promises" (CEV).

Psalm 42 is a Psalm from the descendants of Korah and it also begins in despair: "As the deer longs for streams of water, so I long for you, O God. I thirst for God, the living God. When can I go and stand before him? Day and night I have only tears for food." However, the Psalm ends with optimism: "I will put my hope in God! I will praise him again—my Savior and my God!"

To quote one more example of worry to worship, this Psalm leads with discouragement and maybe even a little anger: "Show that I am right, God! Defend me against everyone who doesn't know you; rescue me from each of those deceitful liars. I run to you for protection. Why have you turned me away? Why must enemies mistreat me and make me sad?" Still, the Psalm ends with trust and praise: "Why am I discouraged? Why am I restless? I trust you! And I will praise you again because you help me, and you are my God" (43:1-2, 5 CEV).

Never allow satan to pile guilt on top of your pain by making you believe you aren't godly if you feel grief. However, do grieve with hope, and work towards turning your pain into praise. The Lord says there is a time for everything: "For everything there is a season, a time for every activity under heaven. A time to be born and a time to die. A time to plant and a time to harvest. A time to kill and a time to heal. A time to tear down and a time to build up. A time to cry and a time to laugh. *A time to grieve and a time to dance*" (Ecclesiastes 3:1-4, emphasis added).

The Book of Ruth relates the story of a woman named Naomi who suffered great loss and heartbreak. She lived in a foreign land with her husband, two sons and their wives, until her husband and sons all died. In despair, she decided to return to her people (this can be an encouragement for us to seek the help of those who know us best during our times of need). Her daughter-in-law, Ruth, went with her and together they began new lives.

Naomi traveled a tough road, and during her journey she had to work through the pain of her grief. Deeply mourning, she desired to change her name from Naomi, which means "sweet, pleasant," to Mara, which means "bitterness." Upon her arrival home, she told the townspeople:

> "Don't call me Naomi," she responded. 'Instead, call me Mara, for the Almighty has made my life very bitter for me. I went away full, but the Lord has brought me home empty. Why call me Naomi when the Lord has caused me to suffer and the Almighty has sent such tragedy upon me?" (Ruth 1:20–21)

However, in due season, through her grave sorrow came great blessings from the Lord. Joy was restored to both Naomi and Ruth, and God's purpose was fulfilled when Ruth became a part of the lineage of Jesus Christ through her marriage to Boaz.

As those in the Bible have shown us, there is a time for grieving and a time to move on. David mourned the death of the child born through his sin with Bathsheba in a manner different from the death of his son, Absalom. When the child became sick after the Lord had already predicted his death:

> David prayed to God for the baby. David refused to eat or drink. He went into his house and stayed there and lay on the ground all night.
>
> The leaders of David's family came and tried to pull David up from the ground, but he refused to get up. He refused to eat with these leaders. On the seventh day the baby died. David's servants were afraid to tell him that the baby was dead. They said, "Look, we tried to talk to David while the baby was alive, but he refused to listen to us. If we tell David that the baby is dead, he might do something bad to himself."
>
> David saw his servants whispering and understood that the baby was dead. So David asked his servants, "Is the baby dead?"

The servants answered, "Yes, he is dead."

Then David got up from the floor. He washed himself. He changed his clothes and got dressed. Then he went into the Lord's house to worship. After that he went home and asked for something to eat. His servants gave him some food, and he ate.

David's servants asked him, "Why are you doing this? When the baby was alive, you cried and refused to eat. But when the baby died you got up and ate food."

David said, "While the baby was still living, I cried and refused to eat because I thought, 'Who knows? Maybe the Lord will feel sorry for me and let the baby live.' But now the baby is dead, so why should I refuse to eat? Can I bring the baby back to life? No. *Someday I will go to him, but he cannot come back to me.*" (2 Samuel 12:16-23 ERV, emphasis added)

During the time the child was sick, David went through a period of repentance, praying the Lord would change His mind. But when that didn't happen, David accepted God's answer through the grace and comfort of knowing one day he and his child would be reunited.

When people go through trials, a verse that's often used to offer comfort is Romans 8:28: "And we know that God causes everything to work together for the good of those who love God and are called according to his purpose for them." There are times when that Scripture will give us great peace, but the verse can also be upsetting during moments when we wonder how such a thing could possibly be true.

Tsunamis

However, the Lord really can cause the sun to shine through the stormiest of days. The death of Jesus is proof. The torture of Jesus' flesh being ripped open, His agonizing walk to Calvary, the stakes being driven through His hands and feet, the horror of His Father turning away, His painful death, and the spear piercing His side…all happened to Someone who was falsely accused and didn't deserve to die. Yet God planned it. The Lord allowed evil in order to bring about His purpose: defeating death and sin, and giving us the opportunity for eternal life with God. The darkest moment in history, but the Son shone through. Each of your storms hold the promise of a rainbow too. The Lord will be with you through it all, your Comforter and Deliverer. Trust that He is in control of your life.

1 Samuel shares the story of Hannah, a woman who grieved tremendously over her lack of fertility. To add salt to the wound, her husband's other wife had children and she taunted Hannah until Hannah was reduced to tears and wouldn't eat. On top of that, her husband didn't understand her grief. Beside herself, Hannah poured out her heart to God:

> Hannah was in deep anguish, crying bitterly as she prayed to the Lord. And she made this vow: "O Lord of Heaven's Armies, if you will look upon my sorrow and answer my prayer and give me a son, then I will give him back to you. He will be yours for his entire lifetime, and as a sign that he has been dedicated to the Lord, his hair will never be cut."
> (1:10-11)

Hannah battled a fierce storm but she remembered to pray. While the waves of arrogance and misunderstanding from others washed over her, she kept her head down and her faith up.

> When Elkanah slept with Hannah, the Lord remembered her plea, and in due time she gave birth to a son. She named him Samuel, for she said, "I asked the Lord for him." (1:19-20)

Hannah experienced a time of grieving, but the Lord eventually honored her prayers.

Nevertheless, for reasons known only to Him, the Lord doesn't always answer our prayers in the way we want Him to. You may never give birth to a child, reunite with your spouse, or accomplish your dreams. But you *can* receive comfort from the One who understands your pain and heartache, who suffered great loss, and who also wept. "He was despised and rejected—a man of sorrows, acquainted with deepest grief" (Isaiah 53:3).

When waves of grief overpower and praying seems pointless, pray anyway. When reading the Bible is the last thing you want to do, make it the first thing you do. Find even the smallest thing to be thankful for and praise the Lord. Realize your "why" questions may never get answered this side of heaven. Instead, rejoice in Who you know and not what you know.

Grieving is natural but it does have an expiration date. "Weeping may last through the night, but joy comes with the morning" (Psalm 30:5).

Allow your grief to give you a new outlook on life and remind you of what's really important. Let go of past expectations so you don't lose your perspective for the future.

Thankfully, grief won't last forever. The Lord promises there will be a day when "He will wipe every tear from [your] eyes, and there will be no more death or sorrow or crying or pain. All these things are gone forever" (Revelation 21:4).

Hallelujah—what a glorious day that will be!

Tsunamis

PRAYER

Heavenly Father, when my heart is broken, thank You for picking up the pieces and putting me back together again. Please bring friends into my life to share my heartaches and help me overcome. In turn, use me to bring comfort to others. Rescue me when I flounder too long under the waves of grief. Turn my face from the sand to the sky so I can sense Your glorious Light. Jesus, I pray for You to wrap Your loving arms around me and give me a peace that surpasses all understanding. Thank You, Lord, for promising that those who mourn will be comforted. In the name of Jesus, My Comforter, I pray, Amen!

CHAPTER 6

TORNADOES
Green Skies of Envy and Jealousy

Anger is cruel, and wrath is like a flood, but jealousy is even more dangerous (Proverbs 27:4).

The sound of howling wind drowns out all screams. On the dark, greenish horizon a massive funnel descends from a cloud and touches the ground, spinning furiously towards the farm. Chickens scurry around and horses run away. The girl rushes to the safety of her home, but when she opens the screen door it is ripped from its hinges and blows away. Amid the noise like a freight train, the house is swept up into the twister and Dorothy is no longer in Kansas.

The tornado scene in the classic film, *The Wizard of Oz* is terrifying. One unforgettable moment for me as a child was when the horrible neighbor, Miss Gulch, is seen pedaling her bicycle through the air inside the funnel cloud and then suddenly transforms into a cackling witch on a broomstick.

The most violent of atmospheric storms, tornadoes scare me much more than hurricanes. With a hurricane there are days and sometimes even weeks to prepare, but a tornado often strikes without warning. Even during occasions when the skies turn green and the air is eerily calm prior to the sighting of a twister, there is still little time to prepare before the rotating mass of destructive air hits.

Jealousy and envy are often instantaneous emotions. They strike with little warning. A friend drives up in a luxurious new car. Someone babbles on about the love of her life while you're still waiting to find yours. A co-worker gets offered more money to work at a bigger company and you're still grinding away unnoticed and unappreciated.

These powerful emotions existed even before the creation of man. During his time as an angel, satan became filled with envy (and pride), and he plotted to take over God's job. Satan said, "I'll climb to heaven. I'll set my throne over the stars of God. I'll run the assembly of angels that meets on sacred Mount Zaphon. I'll climb to the top of the clouds. I'll take over as King of the Universe!" (Isaiah 14:13 MSG).

Envy also caused tragedy to strike the very first family. Cain and Abel, two siblings of Adam and Eve, brought their offerings before the Lord and the Lord preferred Abel's sacrifice. Even though Abel had put more thought into his offering, Cain was struck with envy and killed his brother.

While Cain's actions may seem extreme, envy and jealousy have been motivating factors in countless murders throughout time. The news is regularly filled with stories of murderous ex-lovers who became jealous when the other person found new love. One woman, after discovering her ex-boyfriend was dating someone else, laughed as she threw a glass of 98 percent proof sulfuric acid at him, saying "If I can't have you, no one else can."[1]

Another woman burned her neighbors to death because she envied the couple's happiness. She suffered a turbulent relationship with her own boyfriend and apparently resented her neighbors' stable relationship. She set their apartment on fire and the blaze not only killed the couple, but three children who were also in the apartment that night.[2]

Along with relationship envy and jealousy, envy over another person's achievements and material possessions is a murderous driving force for some. A sixteen-year-old girl was stabbed forty-nine times by her cousin, who then ripped the coveted pair of tennis shoes off her feet and stole her electronic gadgets.[3]

The Bible tells the story about Joseph's brothers who became so envious of Joseph for being the favored son that they threw him into a pit and were prepared to let him die. One of the triggers was a multi-colored coat given to Joseph by his father. "Jacob gave him a special coat, which was long and very beautiful. When Joseph's brothers saw that their father loved Joseph more than he loved them, they hated their brother because of this" (Genesis 37:3-4).

Most of us never go to those extremes, but the twister inside of us can cause great health and mental challenges, and even damage lives. When envy (wanting something someone else has and usually resenting that person for it) and jealousy (the fear of losing what you have) are mixed with feelings such as anger, fear, depression, and anxiety, they make an especially toxic combination.

Combining jealousy and envy with bitterness can cause relationships to be lost. Jealousy and anger can lead to abuse. Our bodies take a serious beating: stress lowers the immune system; headaches, insomnia, and digestive problems can develop; blood pressure goes up and so does the risk for heart attacks; and feelings of hopelessness or unworthiness can lead to depression.

The Bible warns: "Peace of mind makes the body healthy, but jealousy is like a cancer" (Proverbs 14:30 ERV). It also says: "Envy and jealousy will kill a stupid fool" (Job 5:2 CEV).

After David killed Goliath, the women from all the towns of Israel came before King Saul singing and dancing. They sang, "Saul has slain his thousands, and David his ten thousands!" (1 Samuel 18:7).

King Saul turned green with envy. "What's this?" he said. "They credit David with ten thousands and me with only thousands" (8).

Alarmed his kingdom would be taken away from him, King Saul also became extremely jealous. The Bible says, "So from that time on Saul kept a jealous eye on David" (8).

Saul's jealousy, anger, envy, and fear intensified. He wasted time chasing David instead of concentrating on the kingdom. Those emotions drove Saul to madness. "[H]e began to rave in his house like a madman. David was playing the harp, as he did each day. But Saul had a spear in his hand, and he suddenly hurled it at David, intending to pin him to the wall" (10-11).

In the end, King Saul committed suicide.

The Bible says, "Whenever people are jealous or selfish, they cause trouble and do all sorts of cruel things" (James 3:16 CEV). Jealousy and envy cause us to focus on the wrong things. Often our perception gets misconstrued. We act in ways we normally wouldn't.

"But if your heart is full of bitter jealousy and selfishness, don't brag or lie to cover up the truth. That kind of wisdom doesn't come from above. It is earthly and selfish and comes from the devil himself" (James 3:14-15 CEV).

Envy over someone else's property caused King Ahab to commit an evil act. Ahab coveted a vineyard belonging to Naboth and offered to buy it, but Naboth refused. The property was an inheritance from Naboth's ancestors and the Lord had expressly forbidden the sale of that land. Ahab whined and his wife, Jezebel, took matters into her own hands. She ordered Naboth to be stoned to death on a falsified charge of blasphemy. The envious king received his vineyard, but years later Jezebel was killed and dogs ate her body on that same plot of ground. A high price was paid for their covetous ways (1 Kings 21). The Bible cautions:

> You must not want to take your neighbor's house. You must not want his wife. And you must not want his men and women servants or his cattle or his donkeys. *You must not want to take anything that belongs to another person.* (Exodus 20:17 ERV, emphasis added)

The workplace is an atmosphere ripe for tornadoes. Co-workers are envious when someone else is praised by the boss, gets promoted, or makes more money, and this creates a swirl of office gossip, loss of productivity, and lack of teamwork. Galatians 6:4 advises: "Pay careful attention to your own work, for then you will get the satisfaction of a job well done, and you won't need to compare yourself to anyone else."

While it's ultimately a story about the Kingdom of Heaven and God's unmerited grace, The Parable of the Workers in the Vineyard (Matthew 20) reflects many workplace atmospheres. Early one morning a landowner went out and hired workers for his vineyard. He told them he would pay the normal daily wage and the laborers agreed. At nine o'clock in the morning, at noon, and again at three p.m. the landowner hired more workers for the vineyard, agreeing to also pay them a fair wage. At five p.m. the landowner hired yet another group of laborers and sent them into the vineyard. When evening came, the boss paid everyone the same amount. Those who had been working since early morning complained it wasn't fair for the others to be paid as much as them when they hadn't worked as long:

> He [the vineyard owner] answered one of them, "Friend, I haven't been unfair! Didn't you agree to work all day for the usual wage? Take your money and go. I wanted to pay this last worker the same as you. Is it against the law for me to do what I want with my money? Should you be jealous because I am kind to others?" (13-14)

Speaking out against others because of envy or jealousy is not how we are to conduct ourselves, even when we feel it isn't fair. In the workplace (and in all arenas of life) we should do our best to follow the instructions given in Philippians 2:

> If you've gotten anything at all out of following Christ, if his love has made any difference in your life, if being in a community of the Spirit means anything to you, if you have a heart, if you *care*—then do me a favor: Agree with each other, be deep-spirited friends. Don't push your way to the front; don't sweet talk your way to the top. Put yourself aside, and help others get ahead. Don't be obsessed with getting your own advantage. Forget yourselves long enough to lend a helping hand. (1-4 MSG)

Jealousy even reigns in ministry. Paul and Barnabas dealt with it while they were ministering. "The following week almost the entire city turned out to hear them preach the word of the Lord. *But when some of the Jews saw the crowds, they were jealous, so they slandered Paul and argued against whatever he said*" (Acts 13:44-46, emphasis added).

The conditions of social media can also be conducive to creating a tornado. Seeing our friends posting pictures from Disney World and the beach while we are stuck cleaning the house can cause green skies of envy. A long awaited day relaxing alone at the pool with a good book suddenly seems lonely when we notice posts of couples enjoying the day together.

Even though it may look like everyone else has a more exciting social life, we all have our share of uneventful days. Keep in mind, things are not always what they seem to be. People may be smiling pretty for pictures, but might be an unhappy mess inside. "Let us not become conceited, or provoke one another, or be jealous of one another" (Galatians 5:26).

Most of us at some time or another have probably felt the "green-eyed monster" trying to creep up on us. Experiencing continued jealousy and envy, however, will lead to a spirit of discontentment. It's possible for dissatisfaction with life to turn into depression, which can be dangerous. Suicides are increasing at an alarming rate. Incidentally, many suicide victims seemed to "have it all," but still took their own lives. Money, fame, beauty, the supposedly perfect spouse or children … none of these will fulfill you. Only Jesus can.

King Solomon, the richest man in the world, enjoyed every pleasure under the sun, but without the Lord for a season, and he discovered: "There was nothing really worthwhile anywhere" (Ecclesiastes 2:11). A life not filled with God will always be empty.

When I get stuck in a rut and feel my life is monotonous, I start imagining what other people might be doing with their day and the Lord inevitably brings to my mind those who are confronting worse conditions than my doldrums: people sitting in a hospital room with a terminally ill child; a person mourning the loss of a loved one; individuals who can't hear or see or walk; someone who is tiptoeing on eggshells to avoid a beating; and those who don't know where they're going to sleep tonight. I suddenly realize how blessed I am, and the envy monster begins to retreat.

There are always going to be people with more than you and there will also be people with less. It's the math of life. When things don't seem to be adding up, that's when you need to rely on God to help you use your discontentment to change your circumstances. But if your circumstances can't be changed, then changing your attitude will at least make life a little rosier (instead of green).

While envy is dangerous because of the resentment involved, jealousy is not always bad. In fact, the Bible informs us God Himself is a jealous God. The Lord commanded in Exodus:

> You must not make for yourself an idol of any kind or an image of anything in the heavens or on the earth or in the sea. You must not bow down to them or worship them, *for I, the* Lord *your God, am a jealous God who will not tolerate your affection for any other gods.* (Exodus 20:4-5, emphasis added)

The Bible also says, "You must worship no other gods, for the Lord, whose very name is Jealous, is a God who is jealous about his relationship with you" (Exodus 34:14).

The Lord is jealous because we belong to Him. We were created for God and He wants us. Our hearts should belong to Him and He is rightfully jealous when we put other things before Him. He loves us and is jealous *for* us with a protective, righteous jealousy. The Apostle Paul describes godly jealousy in 2 Corinthians: "I am jealous for you with a jealousy that comes from God. I promised to give you to Christ. He must be your only husband. I want to give you to Christ to be his pure bride" (11:2 ERV).

Jealousy can be good when it's used in the proper way to hold onto what is rightful ours, when we use it for self-improvement, and when it draws us closer to the Lord.

However, the dark side of jealousy and envy will cast a shadow over our spiritual lives and pull us away from God. We become preoccupied with the things of this world instead of the righteousness of the Lord. We open doors to things that will rot our souls rather than lift our spirits. When we close the door to God, Ecclesiastes 4:4 points out: "And I saw that all toil and all achievement spring from one person's envy of another. This too is meaningless, a chasing after the wind" (NIV).

The Bible tells us to be content with what we have: "Yet true godliness with contentment is itself great wealth" (1 Timothy 6:6). Being jealous or envious brings into question our trust in God's plan and implies we aren't satisfied with His blessings.

The way to survive the ferocity of jealousy and envy is to strive to be more like Christ. Love as He loves. 1 Corinthians 13:4-5 says: "Love is patient, love is kind. It does not envy, it does not boast, it is not proud. It does not dishonor others, it is not self-seeking, it is not easily angered, it keeps no record of wrongs" (NIV). Focus less on self and more on Jesus. Gain new perspective by getting involved in volunteering and helping others in need. When we take our eyes off the things of this world and look to Jesus, jealousy and envy loosen their grip on us.

The Bible instructs:
> So behave properly, as people do in the day. Don't go to wild parties or get drunk or be vulgar or inde-

cent. Don't quarrel or be jealous. Let the Lord Jesus
Christ be as near to you as the clothes you wear.
Then you won't try to satisfy your selfish desires.
(Romans 13:13-14 CEV)

Gratitude and humility overpower jealousy and envy. Identify your triggers and try to avoid them. Take a break from social media, the internet and television if they are creating a twister. Set your eyes on Kingdom treasures instead of earthly possessions. The Bible says, "Stop being hateful! Quit trying to fool people, and start being sincere. Don't be jealous or say cruel things about others. Be like newborn babies who are thirsty for the pure spiritual milk that will help you grow and be saved (1 Peter 2:1-2 CEV).

There's no need to be envious of anyone because you are as precious to God as anybody else. He might just have a different plan for your life. So, even though you may wish for another person's long legs, straight nose, curly hair, fat wallet, loving spouse, big house, dream job, or quiet children, count the blessings in your own life. You can bet someone else is!

When I went through a divorce from my children's father, I suddenly found myself a single mom to three young kids. In the beginning, I remember feeling envious when I'd watch a beautiful family with both mom and dad holding onto their children's hands as they strolled into church together, while I struggled to hold one child in my arms as the other two grasped onto my skirt. Or at restaurants when I'd see a mom who was able to take one child to the bathroom while the father stayed at the table with the rest, instead of dragging all the children with her into one stall.

After a while, though, I began to realized what a blessing my alone time was with my children. We formed a tight bond as I was able to focus on them in ways I wouldn't have been able to had my attention been divided. We satisfied our days with outreach ministry and mission trips. Our nights were filled with board games, popcorn fights, and dance parties—and when bad dreams scared them awake, there was plenty of room for them to crawl into bed with me.

Given a choice, of course I would rather have stayed an intact family unit, but the Lord showed me there was no need to envy what I didn't have because He gives in abundance in other ways.

Our new lifestyle taught us to be flexible and spontaneous: to simply enjoy life and each other. Although money was tight, it allowed us to grasp the concept that "[i]t is better to be happy with what you have than to always want more and more. Always wanting more and more is useless. It is like trying to catch the wind" (Ecclesiastes 6:9 ERV). We learned to fully trust the Lord to provide.

God gave us life lessons beyond green skies and more valuable than any yellow brick road.

The Lord tells us that one day there will be a new heaven and a new earth where envy or jealousy won't exist because "nothing unworthy will be allowed to enter" (Revelations 21:27). There will be no occasions for such emotions. All believers will get to live in a bejeweled city and walk on a street of pure gold. Revelations describes the new Jerusalem:

> The wall was made of jasper. The city was made of pure gold, as pure as glass. The foundation stones of the city walls had every kind of expensive jewels in them. The first foundation stone was jasper, the second was sapphire, the third was chalcedony, the fourth was emerald, the fifth was onyx, the sixth was carnelian, the seventh was yellow quartz, the

eighth was beryl, the ninth was topaz, the tenth was chrysoprase, the eleventh was jacinth, and the twelfth was amethyst. The twelve gates were twelve pearls. Each gate was made from one pearl. The street of the city was made of pure gold, as clear as glass. (Revelations 21:18-21 ERV)

Most importantly though, we will all be basking in His radiant love. "And the city has no need of sun or moon, for the glory of God illuminates the city, and the Lamb is its light" (Revelations 21:23).

Banish the green-eyed monster by thanking the Lord for the things you've been given, and praising Him for the things to come.

PRAYER

Heavenly Father, when my skies turn green and I feel jealousy and envy twisting inside me, please be my storm cellar—a safe place to gain new perspective and peace. Help me to quickly overcome the desire to have what someone else has and instead be thankful for the blessings You've given me. Whatever my lot in life is, I trust You to use it for Your glory. Help me to not compare my life to others. Forgive me for the times when I've let jealousy and envy rear their ugly heads. Through You, I can tame the green-eyed monster! In the name of Jesus, One Who Sets Free, I pray, Amen!

CHAPTER 7

OVERCAST
Effects of Illness

He heals the brokenhearted and binds up their wounds (Psalm 147:3 NIV).

If you are suffering from any type of illness, every single day seems overcast. When your strength is evaporating and agony pours down, it's hard to focus on anything else. Your storm may be the light shower of flu or a thunderstorm of cancer or other life-threatening disease. When your body is sick, everything else suffers too.

Not feeling well is one of life's biggest distractions. When muscles and joints ache, it's hard to get moving. Nausea, dizziness, shortness of breath, and foggy brain all keep us focused on our symptoms. Researching ailments on the internet consume our time, and then all the dreary forecasts keep us awake at night.

Illness can also threaten our relationship with the Lord when we begin to doubt He cares. "Why then does my suffering continue? Why is my wound so incurable? Your help seems as uncertain as a seasonal brook, like a spring that has gone dry" (Jeremiah 15:18).

You are not alone in your suffering. Illness and disease are rampant in our fallen world. Can God heal you? Yes, He can. He is Jehovah-Rapha (the Lord who heals). Will He? Not always. But He does promise to always be with you.

We are imperfect beings living in a fallen world filled with diseases, bacteria, and viruses that invade our bodies. We have an enemy who wants to oppress us with illness. Thankfully, we serve a compassionate God who is with us during our times of sickness. The comforting hand of Jesus will hold onto believers who must travel a path of pain, and when we walk with Him we can endure.

The Bible reveals how the Lord uses different approaches to healing: sometimes a person is made well through faith, sometimes through divine healing, and there are times when the Lord doesn't heal a person in the physical sense this side of heaven.

The Scriptures mention many instances where people were healed through their faith. Matthew 9:27-30 relates a time when Jesus encountered two blind men along His travels:

> After Jesus left the girl's home, two blind men followed along behind him, shouting, "Son of David, have mercy on us!"
>
> They went right into the house where he was staying and Jesus asked them, "Do you believe I can make you see?"
>
> "Yes, Lord," they told him, "we do."
>
> Then he touched their eyes and said, *"Because of your faith, it will happen."* Then their eyes were opened and they could see!" (emphasis added)

Another time a blind beggar named Bartimaeus sat by the road near Jesus. He started shouting, "Jesus, Son of David, have mercy on me!"

Many people yelled at him to stop, but he shouted even louder and caught the attention of Jesus, who asked him to come over. The blind man approached Jesus and Jesus asked him what he wanted. The blind man told Jesus he wanted to see.

"And Jesus said to him, '*Go, for your faith has healed you.*' Instantly the man could see, and he followed Jesus down the road" (Mark 10:46-52, emphasis added).

One of the most well-known stories of faith healing is the woman with constant bleeding. For twelve years she suffered without a cure. One day she fought her way through a crowd and snuck up behind Jesus to touch the fringe of His robe. Her bleeding immediately stopped. Jesus asked who touched Him because He felt healing power go out of Him. The woman fell on her knees before Him and confessed.

"Daughter," he said to her, "*your faith has made you well.* Go in peace" (Luke 8:48, emphasis added).

When we are weak during moments of suffering we may question our circumstances and our faith. To make matters worse, sometimes others will tell us if we just had enough faith we'd be healed. According to Scripture, however, faith is not always a prerequisite to receive healing. Sometimes faith follows the miracle.

One such instance is recorded in Luke 7:11-15 when Jesus and his disciples went to the village of Nain:

> A funeral procession was coming out as he [Jesus] approached the village gate. The young man who had died was a widow's only son, and a large crowd from the village was with her. When the Lord saw

her, his heart overflowed with compassion. "Don't cry!" he said. Then he walked over to the coffin and touched it, and the bearers stopped. "Young man," he said, "I tell you, get up." Then the dead boy sat up and began to talk! And Jesus gave him back to his mother.

No one expected Jesus to show up, there was no anticipation of healing and no profession of faith ahead of time. The miracle came first.

Another example is found in the Book of Acts when on their way to the temple, Peter and John saw a lame man begging for money. Peter told the man to look at them and the man did, expecting to receive money. Instead Peter told the beggar:

"I don't have any silver or gold for you. But I'll give you what I have. In the name of Jesus Christ the Nazarene, get up and walk!'

Then Peter took the lame man by the right hand and helped him up. And as he did, the man's feet and ankles were instantly healed and strengthened. He jumped up, stood on his feet, and began to walk! Then, walking, leaping, and praising God, he went into the Temple with them." (Acts 3:1-8)

The lame man expected money, not healing. Instead he received healing, and his faith followed as he praised the Lord.

Don't believe you aren't healed simply because you don't have enough faith. There are pastors, evangelists, missionaries, and many other godly people who have not been healed. Even men of the Bible suffered illness. The Apostle Paul told Timothy, another mighty servant of God: "Don't drink only water. You ought to drink a little wine for the sake of your stomach because you are sick so often" (1 Timothy 5:23). Paul also "left Trophimus sick at Miletus" (2 Timothy 4:20).

Not only is lack of faith used to explain the absence of healing at times, but others may also tell you it must be because of sin in your life (adding guilt now to your list of ailments). Job's "friends" did just that when they told him:

> "Stop and think! Do the innocent die? When have the upright been destroyed? My experience shows that those who plant trouble and cultivate evil will harvest the same. A breath from God destroys them.... But look, God will not reject a person of integrity, nor will he lend a hand to the wicked."
> (4:7-9; 8:20)

Not exactly helpful support! Even though the Bible does give examples of sickness being inflicted because of sin, the Bible also reveals that's not always the case and shouldn't be assumed. Not only did God rebuke Job's friends for speaking falsely, but the Gospel of John recounts a time when Jesus healed a blind man and corrected the disciples' assumption about sin and sickness:

> As Jesus was walking along, he saw a man who had been blind from birth. "Rabbi," his disciples asked him, *"why was this man born blind? Was it because of his own sins or his parents' sins?"*
>
> *"It was not because of his sins or his parents' sins,"* Jesus answered. *"This happened so the power of God could be seen in him."* (John 9:1-3, emphasis added)

Instead of questioning whether you are being punished or if you failed God, use this storm to grow closer to the Lord. Confess any sins and gain godly perspective by trusting that no matter the source, God is in control and will use your situation for His glory.

The Psalmist understood how the Lord can use suffering to achieve righteousness in our lives when he said: "Before I was afflicted I went astray, but now I obey your word" (Psalm 119:67 NIV).

Believe the Lord can heal who He wants when He wants, but remember the decision is His to make. Even so, we should still be inspired to pray for healing. In the Book of Second Kings, King Hezekiah prayed to the Lord when he was about to die and the Lord changed His mind and healed Hezekiah:

> About that time Hezekiah became deathly ill, and the prophet Isaiah son of Amoz went to visit him. He gave the king this message: "This is what the Lord says: Set your affairs in order, for you are going to die. You will not recover from this illness."
>
> When Hezekiah heard this, he turned his face to the wall and prayed to the Lord "Remember, O Lord, how I have always been faithful to you and have served you single-mindedly, always doing what pleases you." Then he broke down and wept bitterly.
>
> But before Isaiah had left the middle courtyard, this message came to him from the Lord: "Go back to Hezekiah, the leader of my people. Tell him, 'This is what the Lord, the God of your ancestor David, says: *I have heard your prayer and seen your tears. I will heal you, and three days from now you will get out of bed and go to the Temple of the Lord. I will add fifteen years to your life,* and I will rescue you and this city from the king of Assyria....'"
>
> Then Isaiah said, "Make an ointment from figs." So Hezekiah's servants spread the ointment over

the boil, *and Hezekiah recovered*! (20:1-7, emphasis added)

Faithfully pray for healing, then trust in God's sovereign wisdom.

God honors the prayers of His people but He doesn't always honor them the way we want Him to. Sometimes He grants healing through doctors or other earthly methods, sometimes through a miracle, and sometimes the ultimate healing is rewarded in Heaven.

Even when our prayers for healing seem to go unanswered and our finite minds don't understand the will of God, the Lord will give us the grace to proclaim: "We can rejoice, too, when we run into problems and trials, for we know that they help us develop endurance. And endurance develops strength of character, and character strengthens our confident hope of salvation. And this hope will not lead to disappointment. For we know how dearly God loves us, because he has given us the Holy Spirit to fill our hearts with his love" (Romans 5:3-5).

Sometimes God's people will suffer. The most powerful example of someone of faith who suffered is the beating and crucifixion of Jesus Christ. Stripped of His clothing, with His hands bound upright to a post, Jesus was scourged over and over again with flagellums. These whips had several strands weighted with sharp pieces of sheep bones or lead balls. The strands and bones lacerated His skin, while the lead balls caused deep welts. Pieces of flesh ripped open and blood flowed. The violent beatings continued to the brink of death. A crown of thorns pierced Jesus' head and blood ran down His face. Placed on the cross with His shredded back against the pole, nails were pounded into His hands and feet. Jesus hung in excruciating pain, cut off from His Father's presence as He suffered an agonizing death. If God allowed His sinless Son to experience that torture, who are we to question our own fate?

No matter what happens, we have the promise that it's not the end. 1 Corinthians 15:55 says, "Where, O death, is your victory? Where, O death, is your sting?" All believers will one day enjoy glorified bodies in Heaven.

Until that time, we live with the fact that the Lord is sovereign and the choice to heal is His. If God's will was for everyone to always be healed here on earth, then no one would ever be sick or die. However, Jesus' main purpose when He came to this world wasn't to heal but "to seek and to save those who are lost" and to be a light, "so that all who put their trust in me will no longer remain in the dark" (Luke 19:10 and John 12:46).

He blesses us with healing when it's part of His plan. We receive peace when we simply trust Him.

For reasons inconceivable to our human minds, when satan approached God about Job, the Lord allowed satan to take Job's health, but not his life. Satan struck Job with terrible boils from head to foot and Job was so miserable he scraped his skin with broken pieces of pottery. Describing his pain, Job said:

> "I, to, have been assigned months of futility, long and weary nights of misery. Lying in bed, I think, 'When will it be morning?' But the night drags on, and I toss till dawn. My body is covered with maggots and scabs. My skin breaks open, oozing with pus." (Job 7:3-5)

Job's wife encouraged him to curse God and die, but this man of great faith replied, "You talk like a foolish woman. Should we accept only good things from the hand of God and never anything bad?" (2:10)

Despite being swept up in a catastrophic storm, Job also said, "Though He slay me, yet will I trust Him" (13:15).

My Job experience came after my daughter was born with birth defects when she could have been born whole. But instead of cursing God, I now thank the Lord for Samantha being the rare one in ten thousand born with encephalocele because the brain matter protruding from her head alerted the doctors to her hydrocephalus, which left untreated can be fatal. Since the pressure of too much cerebrospinal fluid damages brain tissue, timeliness is a factor in limiting the impairments to brain function, and many times hydrocephalus isn't detected right away. Her outer defect allowed her other condition to be treated without delay, minimizing the damage.

Although the Lord allowed these conditions even after I prayed for my baby to be born in perfect health, I chose to thank Him for His merciful hand in her treatment. Like Job, I choose to say, "Yet will I trust Him."

A well-known story in the Old Testament is about three friends named Shadrach, Meshach, and Abednego. Because of their faithfulness to the Lord and refusal to serve other gods, King Nebuchadnezzar gave an order for them to be thrown into a fiery furnace. In the midst of a life-or-death storm, they responded with great hope:

> Shadrach, Meshach, and Abednego replied, "O Nebuchadnezzar, we do not need to defend ourselves before you. If we are thrown into the blazing furnace, the God whom we serve is able to save us. He will rescue us from your power, Your Majesty. *But even if he doesn't*, we want to make it clear to you, Your Majesty, that we will never serve your gods or

worship the gold statue you have set up." (Daniel 3:16-18, emphasis added)

What a positive attitude! Even though it's the Lord's choice by His divine reasoning to give us earthly healing or not, it's our choice to select how we will handle the outcome. Will we accept His grace to endure all things? Or will we live a life of bitterness and misery? Our attitude won't change the outcome but it will change our enjoyment of life.

When we are "me" focused, we tend to forget that God never promised us a pain-free life. In fact, He told us we would face all kinds of storms, but He also assured us: "And after you have suffered a little while, the God of all grace, who has called you to his eternal glory in Christ, will himself restore, confirm, strengthen, and establish you" (1 Peter 5:10). The Lord gives us a wholeness beyond physical healing.

Living a joyful life despite pain and illness requires you to focus on God and not your circumstances. Trust that His ways and His will are best, and have faith that He is right there with you through it all. Jesus suffered the most excruciating pain. He understands and weeps with you.

When dark clouds burst forth and you dodge raindrops of fear, pain, doubt, and weakness, hold onto the Umbrella with steadfastness, knowing Jesus will provide the strength. A day will come when "He will take our weak mortal bodies and change them into glorious bodies like his own, using the same power with which he will bring everything under his control" (Philippians 3:21). There will be no more sickness and we will receive new and improved bodies that will last for eternity!

"Therefore, we do not lose heart. Though outwardly we are wasting away, yet inwardly we are being renewed day by day. For our light and momentary troubles are achieving for us an eternal glory that far outweighs them all" (2 Corinthians 4:16–17 NIV).

PRAYER

Jehovah Rapha, My Healer, when weakness and disease cause my days to be overcast and threaten to steal my joy, please bring healing to my body. And when it is not in Your divine plan to take away my afflictions, please give me the strength to handle it. Jesus, I know You have endured more pain and suffering than I ever will and You weep with me and for me. Thank You that no matter what, as a believer I will have a glorified, painless body in heaven! Lord, I have faith in Your Word and I speak these Scriptures over my illness:

Heal me, Lord, and I will be healed; save me and I will be saved, for you are the one I praise (Jeremiah 17:14 NIV).

O Lord my God, I cried to you for help, and you restored my health. You brought me up from the grave, O Lord. You kept me from falling into the pit of death (Psalm 30:2-3).

But for you who revere my name, the sun of righteousness will rise with healing in its rays. And you will go out and frolic like well-fed calves. (Malachi 4:2 NIV).

"I will give you back your health and heal your wounds," says the Lord (Jeremiah 30:17).

The righteous person faces many troubles, but the Lord come to the rescue each time (Psalm 34:19).

The Lord nurses them when they are sick and restores them to health (Psalm 41:3).

Lord, your discipline is good, for it leads to life and health. You restore my health and allow me to live! (Isaiah 38:16).

Don't trust in your own wisdom, but fear and respect the Lord and stay away from evil. If you do this, it will be like a refreshing drink and medicine for your body (Proverbs 3:7-8 ERV).

He gives power to the weak and strength to the powerless (Isaiah 40:29).

The fact is, it was our suffering he [Jesus] took on himself; he bore our pain. But we thought that God was punishing him, that God was beating him for something he did. But he was being punished for what we did. He was crushed because of our guilt. He took the punishment we deserved, and this brought us peace. We were healed because of his pain (Isaiah 53:4-5 ERV).

Let all that I am praise the Lord; may I never forget the good things he does for me. He forgives all my sins and heals all my diseases, He redeems me from death and crowns me with love and tender mercies. He fills my life with good things. My youth is renewed like the eagles! (Psalm 103:2-5).

Then your salvation will come like the dawn, and your wounds will quickly heal. Your godliness will lead you forward, and the glory of the Lord will protect you from behind (Isaiah 58:8).

The Lord will strengthen him on his bed of illness; You will sustain him on his sickbed (Psalm 41:3 NKJV).

In the name of Jesus, the Great Physician, I pray, Amen!

CHAPTER 8

WILDFIRES
The Heat of Anger

"When you are angry, don't let anger make you sin," and don't stay angry all day. Don't give the devil a way to defeat you (Ephesians 4:26 ERV).

Anger can spread like wildfire, destroying everything in its path—and especially the person starting the flames. Left smoldering, anger can burn us up inside or cause us to erupt like a volcano, spewing forth a deadly cloud of unrighteousness. The Bible says, "In your anger, do not sin" (Ephesians 4:6 NIV). While anger is a natural emotion given to us by God, it's what you do with your anger that determines whether or not it's a sin.

There are many times in the Bible when God got angry, especially in the Old Testament. Since the Lord never sins, His anger is never wrong. His anger is based on justice and love. The Lord gets angry at the evil in people and at things that harm His children or threaten His relationship with them. In the Book of First Kings, the Lord instructed the Israelites not to marry foreigners because they didn't worship the True God and would turn the Israelites' hearts to other gods. Unfortunately, King Solomon didn't obey and not only did he marry foreign women, but he also started worshiping other gods. To make his wives happy, Solomon even built pagan shrines to them. The Lord became very angry with Solomon for turning his heart away from the Lord. He specifically warned Solomon against worshiping other gods, but Solomon didn't listen.

> So now the Lord said to him, "Since you have not kept my covenant and have disobeyed my decrees, I will surely tear the kingdom away from you and give it to one of your servants. But for the sake of your father, David, I will not do this while you are still alive. I will take the kingdom away from your son. And even so, I will not take away the entire kingdom; I will let him be king of one tribe, for the sake of my servant David and for the sake of Jerusalem, my chosen city." (11:11-13)

The Lord exhibited righteous anger and He handled it justly. He punished Solomon for his wrong actions, but God still acted in mercy.

Jesus likewise experienced anger when He knew His enemies would accuse Him if He healed a man's deformed hand on the Sabbath:

> *He looked around at them angrily and was deeply saddened by their hard hearts.* Then he said to the man, 'Hold out your hand.' So the man held out his hand, and it was restored! At once the Pharisees went away and met with the supporters of Herod to plot how to kill Jesus." (Mark 3:5-6, emphasis added)

Jesus also became angry when He saw merchants and money dealers misusing the Temple. He made a whip and chased them from the Temple. He even turned over the tables, scattered the money, and drove out the sheep and cattle. He told them, "Stop turning my Father's house into a marketplace!" (John 2:16).

As Christians, there are countless things in this world that should make us angry: the killing of innocent lives and unborn babies, sex trafficking, robbing and violence, starving and abused children, school shootings, disease, and an overwhelming myriad of injustices. It's okay to be angry for just causes, but our anger should be used to inspire us to help change the world.

What about when people personally wrong us though? When others lie to us, gossip about us, rob, cheat, bully or betray us, it's a normal reaction to be angry. As long as we don't exhibit out of control anger, but a controlled burn, our anger can spark regrowth and inspire change. Proverbs 29:11 declares: "A foolish person lets his anger run wild. But a wise person keeps himself under control" (NIRV). The emotion itself is not a sin, but how we handle it can lead to sin. Learning to control our anger is a required life skill.

Nursing a grudge is like keeping an ember of fire licking at your insides. It will consume you first before it damages others. The Bible instructs: "When you are angry, don't let that anger make you sin, and don't stay angry all day. Don't give the devil a way to defeat you" (Ephesians 4:26-27 ERV).

Although you may want to fan the flames and warm yourself by the heat of your bitterness, fueling the fire will only scorch you and give satan an open opportunity to sift through the ashes. Psalm 37:8 warns: "Don't be angry or furious. Anger can lead to sin" (CEV); and Proverbs 29:22 says: "A person with a quick temper stirs up arguments and commits a lot of sins" (CEV).

Uncontrolled anger causes us to take control of situations better left to the Lord. God tells us revenge is for Him to handle. No matter what, all unrighteousness will be judged by God someday, so no one will ultimately get away with anything. If we retaliate against someone else's actions, we'll then have to answer for our own unrighteous acts.

We are to be an example of Christ to others, so we should also handle our anger like Him. The Lord does not hold onto His anger. Micah 7:18-19 says:

> There is no God like you. You take away people's guilt. God will forgive his people who survive. *He will not stay angry with them forever*, because he enjoys being kind. He will come back and comfort us again. He will throw all our sins into the deep ocean. (ERV, emphasis added)

Instead of trying to justify our anger, we should pray for forgiveness and ask God to help us hate the sin but love the person who wronged us.

Jesus is familiar with what we are going through. He knows the pain of betrayal firsthand. One of his very own disciples, Judas, betrayed Him for thirty pieces of silver. "Even my best friend, the one I trusted completely, the one who shared my food, has turned against me" (Psalm 41:9).

Instead of exacting revenge though, after Judas betrayed Him with a kiss, Jesus said, "*My friend*, go ahead and do what you have come for" (Matthew 26:50, emphasis added).

The way for us to keep from fighting fire with fire is to turn to the Lord for strength. He is the One who can put out the flames. It's through the power of Jesus that we can set aside our anger, forgive as He forgives, and love as He loves.

When David had been betrayed by his friends and hunted down by his enemies, instead of being angry and seeking vengeance, he sought the Lord in prayer and came to this conclusion:

Give your burdens to the Lord, *and he will take care of you. He will not permit the godly to slip and fall. But you, O God, will send the wicked down to the pit of destruction. Murderers and liars will die young, but* I am trusting you to save me. (Psalm 55:22-23, emphasis added)

David realized he didn't need to take matters into his own hands. He trusted all-knowing God to see the truth of the situation and to save him, and you can trust the Lord to save you, too.

There are times, though, when we can start a fire and cause the smoke to blow in the wrong direction—straight towards the Lord. All of us have probably had moments in our lives when we've felt angry with God in the midst of a storm. A moment of tragedy sparks the question: "Why, God?"

Brief flickers smoldered in me as I struggled with the reality of my daughter's birth defects:

When I wasn't allowed to hold my baby after she was born.

When I saw her for the first time with wires stuck all over her body and a cap covering her head.

When I wasn't able to feed her for eight hours and listened to her tortured cries.

When I knelt on the cold floor of the hospital bathroom and paced the hallways while she was in surgery—not once, but twice.

When the doctor pointed to the spot on the scan where a part of Samantha's brain should have been.

When the doctor told me my daughter would be mentally and physically impaired but to "just love her."

By the time I was shown the brain scan I couldn't help it any longer and my mind screamed, "Why, God? Why us?" I tried to pray, but felt distant.

At that moment, through the fresh spark of shock and anger, I sensed the Lord speaking to my spirit: "Who do you want it to be?"

It felt like a bucket of cold water being poured on my flames, extinguishing my self-centeredness as I realized I certainly wouldn't want anyone else to suffer this heartbreak. Why should my family be immune to the storms in life that the Lord has already warned us about?

"But my innocent baby…"

"My Son was innocent too, and I watched Him endure great pain."

The verse Jeremiah 29:11 popped into my mind: "'For I know the plans I have for you,' declares the Lord, 'plans to prosper you and not to harm you, plans to give you hope and a future.'"

Suddenly I understood that my anger at God was causing a smokescreen over my faith in His sovereignty. The Creator who formed my little girl still controls the universe.

The embers died and instead of being angry I started focusing on reasons to praise the Lord. Once the smoke cleared and I turned my eyes upward, I discovered there were many.

My daughter thrived when statistically, for those having encephalocele in the back of the skull where Samantha's was, there's only a fifty-five percent survival rate, with a seventy-five percent chance survivors will suffer mental deficits. There is a sixty-percent chance that children with hydrocephalus will require assistance and won't be independent as adults; while just fifty years ago the mortality rate for those with hydrocephalus was extremely high. Only twenty percent of children ever reached adulthood.

The Lord's hand of blessing was clearly on Samantha, and my misplaced anger turned to thankfulness.

But my spark of anger threatened to set off another fire—a wildfire of guilt. Who was I to ignite anger towards the Lord? The devil threatened to burn me up with accusations until I remembered there were many in the Bible who also expressed anger at God. For instance, God's mercy made Jonah angry when God saved the City of Nineveh. Jonah wanted to see the people punished, not saved. Jonah became so angry over the situation that he wanted to die.

Jonah fled and sat down outside the city. It was hot and the Lord caused a plant to grow and shade him. Jonah enjoyed the shelter. But the next day, the Lord sent a worm to eat the plant and it died. The scorching sun and a hot east wind made Jonah miserable. He missed the plant and expressed his anger. God asked Jonah if he had a right to be angry just because a plant died. "Jonah answered, 'Yes, it is right for me to be angry! I am angry enough to die!'" (Jonah 4:9 ERV).

> And the LORD said, "You did nothing for that plant. You did not make it grow. It grew up in the night, and the next day it died. And now you are sad about it. If you can get upset over a plant, surely I can feel sorry for a big city like Nineveh. There are many people and animals in that city. There are more than 120,000 people there who did not know they were doing wrong." (4:10 ERV)

Jonah became so angry with God over the death of a plant and the saving of a nation that he wanted to die. Yet God didn't smite him for his misguided anger, but instead helped Jonah understand the situation.

King David also experienced many times of lashing out:

"O God my rock," I cry, "Why have you forgotten me? Why must I wander around in grief, oppressed by my enemies?" (Psalm 42:9).

"My God, my God, why have you abandoned me? Why are you so far away when I groan for help? Every day I call to you, my God, but you do not answer. Every night I lift my voice, but I find no relief..." (Psalm 22:1-3).

"Wake up, O Lord! Why do you sleep? Get up! Do not reject us forever. Why do you look the other way? Why do you ignore our suffering and oppression?" (Psalm 44:23-24).

Nevertheless, even though David cried out to the Lord in frustration, by the end of each Psalm he always finished his outbursts with praises to the Lord Almighty. This is how we should handle ourselves too. While it's not right to be angry with God because it questions His supreme authority, when we do falter in our humanness and blame God, we should pray for forgiveness and then accept that He understands our frustrations.

Our joy and peace can be restored when we fully trust in the Lord and His perfect plan. Anger, or the guilt of anger, no longer has to rage in our lives. The only remaining flame will be the eternal fire of the Holy Spirit.

PRAYER

Lord God Almighty, I am so thankful You have experienced anger and that You reflect the perfect example of righteous anger. Help me to act instead of react so any anger will be a controlled burn and not a wildfire. Instead of consuming others, let my anger be based on justice and love, and used to bring about change. I pray to be quick to listen, slow to speak and slow to get angry.[1] When I do get angry, keep me from sinning in my anger. God, please fill me with Your calming Spirit. I thank You, Lord, that despite all my sins You never stay angry with me. I love You, Lord! In the name of Jesus, Prince of Peace, I pray, Amen!

CHAPTER 9

TROPICAL DEPRESSION
Finding Joy

...he will give a crown of beauty for ashes, a joyous blessing instead of mourning, festive praise instead of despair... (Isaiah 61:3).

A tropical depression can organize after a set of thunderstorms have joined together under the right atmospheric conditions for a length of time.

Human depression can form under those conditions as well. When storm after storm hits your life, it's easy for your joy to be carried away. It can happen in a catastrophic event or something as simple as losing your keys or picking up a tone of voice in a conversation.

The truth is, most people mistake joy for happiness. But happiness is more reliant on good feelings from external circumstances, while joy is an inner sense of peace and contentment. "In God's kingdom, what we eat and drink is not important. Here is what is important: a right way of life, peace, and joy—all from the Holy Spirit" (Romans 14:17 ERV).

Joy isn't gained through perfect health, a great job, a wonderful spouse, obedient children, and financial stability. Joy also doesn't mean we will always walk on the mountaintops. There will be times of trudging through the valleys. But joy is the consistent feeling that even through the ups and downs of life, we are confident the Lord is in control. Our spirits rest in peaceful assurance that no matter what happens, everything will be all right. This richness of joy is found only in the Lord Jesus Christ.

"You will show me the path of life; in Your presence *is* fullness of joy; at your right hand are pleasures forevermore" (Psalm 16:11 NKJV).

There are times, however, when even Christians are joyless. If you feel you've lost your joy (or maybe you never even found it), you are in company with other godly people in the Bible.

A prophet used mightily by God, Elijah experienced great triumphs through the Lord, but he also battled feelings of defeat. After winning a victory over the prophets of Baal, praying down rain to end the drought, and outrunning a chariot in his zeal, Elijah succumbed to fear over Queen Jezebel's threats to kill him. Forgetting past successes and the power of the Lord in his life, Elijah fled into the wilderness to hide. 1 Kings 19:4 says:

> Then he went on alone into the wilderness, traveling all day. He sat down under a solitary broom tree and prayed that he might die. "I have had enough, Lord," he said. "Take my life, for I am no better than my ancestors who have already died."

Elijah laid down and slept under the tree. While he was sleeping, an angel woke him up and told him to eat. He looked around and there beside him was fresh bread and a jar of water. Elijah had wanted to end his life, but instead the Lord brought him life-giving food and water. After another nap, the angel of the Lord again fed him and Elijah regained his strength enough to travel for forty days and forty nights to Mt. Sinai, where he found a cave.

There at the Mountain of God, Elijah should have basked in God's glory. Instead he hid in the darkness of depression, fear, loneliness, lack of self-worth, and ministry burnout. Elijah lost his joy because he'd taken his focus off the Lord. He forgot he was a servant to All-Mighty God, but the Lord reminded him:

> "Go out and stand before me on the mountain," the Lord told him. And as Elijah stood there, the Lord passed by, and a mighty windstorm hit the mountain. It was such a terrible blast that the rocks were torn loose, but the Lord was not in the wind. After the wind there was an earthquake, but the Lord was not in the earthquake. And after the earthquake there was a fire, but the Lord was not in the fire. And after the fire there was the sound of a gentle whisper. When Elijah heard it, he wrapped his face in his cloak and went out and stood at the entrance of the cave. (11-13)

Discouragement caused Elijah to have a skewed perspective. For one thing, he thought all the other prophets were dead and he was the only one left in ministry. He felt all alone in his faithfulness. Yet Elijah was never alone. The Lord was always right there with him and He ministered to Elijah throughout his wilderness experience.

God restored Elijah to ministry and directed him to go back through the wilderness to Damascus. Along the way, the Lord also showed Elijah his work hadn't been in vain and he wasn't alone in ministry after all—there were 7,000 other faithful Israelites whom the Lord preserved.

Do you ever feel all alone? The Lord hasn't left you either. He is ready to refresh you and call you back into service. Listen carefully though, because His voice might not be in the sensational, but in a gentle whisper that is more audible the closer you are to Him.

Just like God revealed to Elijah there were many other sanctified believers, be assured you aren't the only godly person in the midst of devilish storms either. Elijah's failures didn't end in defeat and neither was his purpose over. God wasn't through with Elijah and He's not through with you!

Jeremiah, the weeping prophet, served the Lord powerfully but still suffered great loneliness and defeat. At times he cursed the day of his birth and questioned, "Why was I ever born? My entire life has been filled with trouble, sorrow, and shame" (Jeremiah 20:18).

King David, a mighty warrior and a man after God's own heart, also experienced many joyless moments. He penned numerous Psalms pouring out his anguish to the Lord. Psalm 142 was written while David sought refuge in a cave from the murderous pursuit of King Saul:

> I cry out to the LORD; I plead for the LORD's mercy.
>
> I pour out my complaints before him and tell him all my troubles.
>
> ...Wherever I go, my enemies have set traps for me.
>
> I look for someone to come and help me, but no one gives me a passing thought! No one will help me; no one cares a bit what happens to me. (1-4)

Psalm 13 is just one more example of David pouring his heart out to the Lord during a time of despair and need:

> O Lord, how long will you forget me? Forever?
> How long will you look the other way?
> How long must I struggle with anguish in my soul, with sorrow in my heart every day? How long will my enemy have the upper hand?
> Turn and answer me, O Lord my God! Restore the sparkle to my eyes, or I will die. (1-3)

The Bible shares David's secret to restoring joy after suffering deep depression: "But David found strength in the Lord his God" (1 Samuel 30:6). Through it all, David rejoiced in the Lord. He poured out his frustrations to God like he would a trusted friend, but David always ended up praising the Lord. He knew where to put his hope, and David had faith in God's love and goodness.

The Lord took care of David and He will take care of you, "for God does not show favoritism" (Romans 2:11). He loves you with the same intense love He had for David. While our moods might change like the wind, God is the same yesterday, today, and forever. Even during the times when you feel like you failed Him, the Lord still loves you with the same passion as the moment He created you. God will never fail you and He will never abandon you.

The Lord tells us over and over again to "fear not." We are not to allow fear and anxiety rule our lives. Storms are joy robbers when we focus too much on our circumstances and not enough on what's beyond the rain. We worry instead of trust. We forget the promises of Jesus because "all too quickly the message is crowded out by the worries of this life, the lure of wealth, and the desire for other things, so no fruit is produced" (Mark 4:19). Joy isn't ours only in the absence of storms. When we look past the clouds to the eternal and praise the Lord regardless, joy can be ours even during trials.

In the Book of Acts, Paul and Silas experienced a breakthrough when they determined to praise Jesus instead of fearing their circumstances. After being beaten with rods and thrown into prison with their feet bound between large blocks of wood, Paul and Silas began worshipping the Lord:

> *About midnight Paul and Silas were praying and singing songs to God.* The other prisoners were listening to them. Suddenly there was an earthquake so strong that it shook the foundation of the jail. All the doors of the jail opened, and the chains on all the prisoners fell off. (22-26 ERV, emphasis added)

Like Paul and Silas, sometimes we have to act joyful even when our circumstances don't warrant it. There is an expression, "pain is inevitable, but misery is optional." When you don't feel like it, "fake it until you make it" and wait for the foundations to be shaken with your breakthrough! The Apostle Paul wrote these words while serving time in prison: "Always be filled with joy in the Lord. I will say it again. Be filled with joy" (Philippians 4:4 ERV).

Remember, our goal is to be filled with lasting joy, not the fleeting emotion of happiness. Galatians 5:22-23 says joy is a fruit of the Spirit: "But the fruit that the Spirit produces in a person's life is love, *joy*, peace, patience, kindness, goodness, faithfulness, gentleness, and self-control" (ERV, emphasis added).

The Spirit is activated through our relationship with Christ, and in the Gospel of John, Jesus shares with us the importance of staying connected to Him:

> *I am the vine, and you are the branches. If you stay joined to me, and I to you, you will produce plenty*

of fruit. But separated from me you won't be able to do anything. If you don't stay joined to me, you will be like a branch that has been thrown out and has dried up. All the dead branches like that are gathered up, thrown into the fire and burned. *Stay joined together with me, and follow my teachings. If you do this, you can ask for anything you want, and it will be given to you.* Show that you are my followers by producing much fruit. This will bring honor to my Father. (15:5-8 ERV, emphasis added)

Jesus then tells us that through our close relationship with Him we will be filled with His joy: "I have told you these things so that you will be filled with my joy. Yes, your joy will overflow!" (John 15:11).

Jesus is the source of our joy.

Like a branch on a vine, we can stay connected to the Lord by reading, believing, and obeying His Word. Trust God's goodness for your life. "Always be joyful. Never stop praying. Be thankful in all circumstances, for this is God's will for you who belong to Christ Jesus" (1 Thessalonians 5:16-18).

Maintain an attitude of gratitude. Appreciate all the Lord has done for you and count your blessings. Resist comparing your circumstances to others. To reiterate a point made in Chapter 6, social media can be a real joy sucker when you start to evaluate your life based on what you see and read about others. Unplug from the internet for a while if necessary and plug into what the Lord has designed for your life. He has a different plan for each of us and you cannot compare yours to someone else's.

Recounting everything the Lord has already done for you is vital to preserving joy. My daughter's birth defects could have been a killjoy had I not been shown the importance of counting my blessings. There's a saying that there's always people worse off than you and it's true, though this is not meant to trivialize what you are going through or invalidate your feelings in any way. Your problems still matter greatly, but your own circumstances are put into perspective when the Lord reveals those persons to you. When that happens, recognize your blessings, pray for those less fortunate, and help them if you are able.

During countless doctor and hospital visits over the years for scans and progress reports, the waiting rooms were always filled with children enduring defects much worse than Samantha's. Some wore helmets on their heads, others lacked mobility, and a number of children had experienced multiple shunt revisions—80 and more! The risk of stroke is high during shunt revisions and many had lost the ability to speak properly due to suffering from strokes. My heart broke as I prayed for every one of them. It also took my eyes off my own issues and onto Jesus and others.

Attending church and fellowshipping with other believers is also important. Build a network of supporters and find ways to use your experiences to help other people who are struggling. Our joy is increased when we share the love of Christ with others, and our problems diminish. It's a God calculation system.

When you are in the middle of an emotional downpour, make time to rest and nourish your body. Don't take your health for granted. Emotional and physical exhaustion will quickly zap your joy. Our minds and bodies need to be renewed. When opposition and pressure wear you down, seek shelter in the Lord. Jesus says, "Come to me all of you who are tired from the heavy burden you have been forced to carry. I will give you rest. Accept my teaching. Learn from me. I am gentle and humble in spirit. And you will be able to get some rest. Yes, the teaching that I ask you to accept is easy. The load I give you to carry is light" (Matthew 11:28-30 ERV).

The inspirational Holocaust survivor, Corrie ten Boom, said: "If you look at the world, you'll be distressed. If you look within, you'll be depressed. But if you look at Christ, you'll be at rest."[1]

Continually praise and worship your King and Savior. Whenever depressing thoughts try to steal your joy, say over and over again: "The joy of the Lord is my strength!" Your words will activate His promises. We are overcomers through the joy of the Lord and can boldly declare: "We are pressed on every side by troubles, but we are not crushed. We are perplexed, but not driven to despair. We are hunted down, but never abandoned by God. We get knocked down, but we are not destroyed!"(2 Corinthians 4:8-9). As Corrie ten Boom said: "There is no pit so deep, that God's love is not deeper still."[1]

Let's remain steadfast in our faith so we can give Christ the same joy He imparts to us: "I have no greater joy than to hear that my children are walking in the truth" (3 John 1:4 NIV).

PRAYER

Heavenly Father, please protect me from the enemy who wants to fill my mind with discouraging thoughts and steal my peace and joy. Instead I bring all of my burdens to You, and I thank You that the joy of the Lord is my strength! I declare no form of worry, depression, anxiety, stress, fear, or sorrow will overtake me. Help me to remember true joy is only found in You. When everything in my life is dark, please shine Your Light. Restore to me the joy of Your salvation and make me willing to obey You.[2] I will no longer be pummeled by tropical depression! In the name of Jesus, My Joy, I pray, Amen!

*While Jesus can heal any affliction, if you are suffering from clinical depression, please seek immediate medical attention and trust the Lord to put into place those in the medical field to help you.

CHAPTER 10

INNER AND OUTER RAINBANDS
Suffering the Effects of Ourselves and Others

> *If you think you can fool God, you are only fooling yourselves. You will harvest what you plant. If you live to satisfy your sinful self, the harvest you will get from that will be eternal death. But if you live to please the Spirit, your harvest from the Spirit will be eternal life* (Galatians 6:7-8 ERV).

Rainbands are dense spiraling bands of thunderstorms and heavy winds. These rainbands have the ability to stay closer to the eye of the storm or to be far-reaching, and the extent of the rainbands impact the intensity of the storm. While the outer rainbands visibly occur outside the inner core, the inner rainbands frequently remain invisible on satellite.

Like outer rainbands, the storms in our lives are often influenced by those around us, but sometimes the storm are inner rainbands that start inside of us.

Even though we may not have control of the life storms that rage around us because of the actions of others, there are times when the adversities are actually brought on by ourselves. Whether it's wrong choices or flat-out disobedience, like a loving parent does to a child, the Lord corrects us. Discipline is never pleasant, but necessary.

We don't punish our children because we hate them, but because of our great love for them. We want them to develop good character and live the best lives possible. The Lord has even more love for His children than earthly parents do and He doesn't delight in punishing us. Rather, He cares too much to stand by and let us continue to mess up our lives. "For the LORD disciplines those he loves, and he punishes each one he accepts as his child" (Hebrews 12:6).

Proverbs also confirms this: "My child, don't reject the LORD's discipline, and don't be upset when he corrects you. For the LORD corrects those he loves, just as a father corrects a child in whom he delights" (3:11-13).

No one appreciates being disciplined at the time, but if the Lord doesn't chastise us when things aren't right, then we should wonder why. His Word warns: "So, if you never receive the discipline that every child must have, you are not true children and don't really belong to God" (Hebrews 12:8 ERV).

In the Book of Numbers, there is a story about a prophet named Balaam who was so eager to follow through on his own plan that He disobeyed God's directive. The king of Moab wanted Balaam to go with his men and pronounce curses on the people of Israel and he offered Balaam a great reward. When Balaam consulted the Lord to see if he could go, the Lord told him: "*If* the men come to call you, rise and go with them…" (22:20 NKJV, emphasis added).

However, in the morning, Balaam apparently saddled up his donkey and went to the men without waiting for them to come to him first. He disobeyed the Lord's directions. God became angry with Balaam and decided to confront him.

As Balaam rode on his donkey, up ahead the Angel of the Lord stood in the way with a drawn sword in his hand. Balaam didn't see the Angel but the donkey did. The donkey turned aside and went into a field to protect his master. Balaam struck the donkey and turned her back onto the road.

A second time the Angel of the Lord stood in their way and again the donkey protected her master, only to suffer another beating. The third time when the Angel of the Lord appeared, the donkey laid down, causing Balaam to hit her yet again.

Then the Lord gave speech to the donkey and the donkey asked Balaam why he struck her three times. Even though the donkey had always been good to Balaam, at that moment Balaam wanted to kill the donkey.

> Then the LORD opened Balaam's eyes, and he saw the Angel of the LORD standing in the way with His drawn sword in His hand; and he bowed his head and fell flat on his face. And the Angel of the LORD said to him, "Why have you struck your donkey these three times? Behold, I have come out to stand against you, because your way is perverse before Me. The donkey saw Me and turned aside from Me these three times. If she had not turned aside from Me, surely I would also have killed you by now, and let her live."
>
> And Balaam said to the Angel of the LORD, "I have sinned, for I did not know You stood in the

way against me. Now therefore, if it displeases You, I will turn back." (Numbers 22:31-34 NKJV)

Three times God allowed the donkey to see the Angel of the Lord, giving Balaam several warnings rather than immediately striking him down for disobeying God. Praise the Lord for His mercy!

The storms in our lives are often sent as a warning also, usually increasing in intensity if the first threatening winds fail to capture our attention. It is smart to heed the advice of Proverbs 22:3: "Wise people see trouble coming and get out of its way, but fools go straight to it and suffer for it" (ERV).

Don't walk straight into an oncoming storm.

King David suffered the consequences of a tragic storm through active sin. First he committed adultery with Bathsheba, then covered up her pregnancy by causing her husband to be killed in battle so he could marry her. David's warning came through the prophet, Nathan, rather than a donkey. Sent by the Lord, Nathan confronted David and prophesied to him the destruction his sin would cause:

> "*So your family will never have peace!* When you took Uriah's wife, you showed that you did not respect me."
>
> "This is what the LORD says: 'I am bringing trouble against you. This trouble will come from your own family. I will take your wives from you and give them to someone who is very close to you. He will have sexual relations with your wives, and everyone will know it! You had sexual relations with Bathsheba in secret, but I will punish you so that all the people of Israel can see it.'"

> Then David said to Nathan, "I have sinned against the LORD."
>
> Nathan said to David, "The LORD will forgive you, even for this sin. You will not die. But you did things that made the LORD's enemies lose their respect for him, so your new baby son will die." (2 Samuel 12:10-14 ERV, emphasis added)

David confessed his sins and the Lord forgave him, but David still suffered the consequences of his sin. The baby died and there never was peace in his family. David's son, Amnon, raped his own sister, Tamar. Another son, Absalom, killed Amnon for raping Tamar. Absalom later took control of David's kingdom, slept with David's wives, and plotted to kill his father. Absalom ended up dying instead and David mourned the loss of another child. Still, through God's mercy and David's repentant attitude, David remained a man after God's own heart and Jesus became a descendant of David.

We can be fooled into thinking our sins are only hurting ourselves when the truth is the effects of our actions are often far-reaching and as devastating as a tsunami after an earthquake, with the ability to destroy everything in its path. At another low point in David's life, his sin cost the lives of 85 priests and the townspeople of Nob. On the run from King Saul, David entered the town of Nob and lied to the high priest, Ahimelech. He tricked Ahimelech into helping him, and when King Saul found out he ordered the death of Ahimelech, along with the others from the town:

> So the king gave the order to Doeg. Saul said, "Doeg, you go kill the priests." So Doeg the Edomite went and killed the priests. That day he killed 85 men who were priests. Nob was the city

of the priests. Doeg killed all the people of Nob. He used his sword and killed men, women, children and small babies. He even killed their cattle, donkeys, and sheep. (1 Samuel 22:18-19 ERV)

It's crucial to look at the big picture when confronted with circumstances. When David lied to Ahimelech, he did so to save himself, without considering his deceit could cost the lives of others.

Sin has a way of revealing itself whether through direct action or through a change in us, but it will not stay hidden. Luke 8:17 warns: "For all that is secret will eventually be brought into the open, and everything that is concealed will be brought to light and made known to all."

Pleasures are fleeting, whereas consequences are long-lasting. Therefore, we should obviously avoid sin and the aftermath of its storms. But when we do get caught up in its torrent, we ought to acknowledge our wrongdoings, confess our sins, and seek forgiveness from the Lord just like David did. We should pray, read His Word, and worship the King of Kings, all the while holding tightly to His umbrella of mercy and rejoicing in the fact that in spite of ourselves, God still loves us.

The word "sin" in the Greek language means to "miss the mark" and we have all done that (or will do that) at times in our lives. The worst magnitude of sin is that it causes us to be separated from the Lord. We serve a holy God and He cannot be in the presence of sin.

Have you ever felt the absence of the Lord? It's an emptiness Jesus dreaded most when faced with His death on the cross. Thankfully, Jesus' blood covers our sins. It cleanses us when we repent and brings us back to a right relationship with the Lord.

Sometimes the guilt of our sins, however, make us feel naked and ashamed before the Lord and causes us to want to hide from

Him as Adam and Eve did. The devil will try to drag you as far away from God as possible by making you believe the Lord is disappointed in you, but the Lord sees beginning to end and whatever happened, God already knew it was coming. You didn't surprise Him, and once you sincerely confess your sins, the Lord forgives you. 1 John 1:9 promises: "But if we confess our sins to him, he is faithful and just to forgive us our sins and to cleanse us from all wickedness."

We don't stop loving our children because they do something wrong, and God doesn't stop loving us either. God demonstrates this in the book of Hosea. The Lord wanted to make a point about the depth of His love for us and he told a man named Hosea to marry a prostitute named Gomer and to have children with her. Hosea did as the Lord told him and they had a son together. Gomer became unfaithful, though, and she bore two other children who were not Hosea's. She left Hosea for other lovers and was eventually sold into slavery.

When Hosea found out what had happened to Gomer he had great compassion for her. His undying love drove him to find her after the Lord directed him: "Go and love your wife again, even though she commits adultery with another lover. This will illustrate that the Lord still loves Israel even though the people have turned to other gods and love to worship them" (3:1). Despite everything Gomer had done, Hosea still bought her back for fifteen shekels of silver and thirteen bushels of barley. He brought Gomer home and she was restored as his wife.

The truth expressed through this poignant love story is that no matter what you've done or didn't do, no matter where you've been, no matter what you might have said to the Lord out of frustration or anger, no matter how far you've wandered from Him,

He still wants you. He will never give up on you and He will never stop loving you!

There are times when we can also get caught in the outer rainbands caused by the sins of other people. The Bible recounts many examples of people who suffered at the hands of others. Abel was killed by his brother, Cain; Joseph was sold as a slave by his brothers; their father, Jacob, mourned the supposed death of his son, Joseph; and Uriah, Bathsheba's husband, was murdered through the instructions of King David. Job even suffered at the hands of satan because of his righteousness. However, the Lord assures us:

> If with heart and soul you're doing good, do you think you can be stopped? Even if you suffer for it, you're still better off. Don't give the opposition a second thought. Through thick and thin, keep your hearts at attention, in adoration before Christ, your Master. Be ready to speak up and tell anyone who asks why you're living the way you are, and always with the utmost courtesy. Keep a clear conscience before God so that when people throw mud at you, none of it will stick. They'll end up realizing that they're the ones who need a bath. It's better to suffer for doing good, if that's what God wants, than to be punished for doing bad. That's what Christ did definitively: suffered because of others' sins, the Righteous One for the unrighteous ones. He went through it all—was put to death and then made alive—to bring us to God. (1 Peter 3:13-18 MSG).

After my daughter, Samantha, was born, I left my employment at the law office so I could be at home with her. We built a daycare center off our house where I ran a successful child care. In fact, it was so successful that I continually had a waiting list. Recognizing the need for another center, we found a charming house with the perfect layout for a daycare not far from our home. I offered one of my employees, a young, single mother with a toddler, the opportunity to move into the house and manage the other daycare. I explained to her the need to maintain an impeccable reputation when operating a child care because people were entrusting us with their most precious treasures, and she assured me she would handle herself appropriately.

I thought I was doing a good thing, but no sooner had we finished putting the colorful blocks and Mr. Potato Heads on the shelves and opened for business than the girl started acting up. She threw wild parties and the neighbors continuously called me to complain. I'd give her a warning, which lasted until the sun went down. Instead of being woken up by my baby, it was the sound of the phone at 3:00 a.m. I really wanted to help this girl have a better life, but after a visit from the police because someone was passed out in the yard and the sun was coming up, I had to shut down the business and remove her from the home. I couldn't believe this person would ruin such a wonderful opportunity and treat me so callously.

Unfortunately, we paid more for the house than we should have because it had been perfect for the daycare and we considered the income it would derive. We struggled to sell it and finally rented the house for lower than our mortgage payments. The extended length of time it took to sell caused financial hardship. Also, part of the joy of opening the second location was to help this young lady and her son. Her utter disregard was disheartening, but all I could do was turn it over to the Lord and move on. We did get through it and I certainly learned to be more discerning.

Sadly, there are people in life who will hurt you. When you suffer for the sins of others though, remember Christ remained innocent, yet suffered for our sins:

> This is the kind of life you've been invited into, the kind of life Christ lived. He suffered everything that came his way so you would know that it could be done, and also know how to do it, step-by-step.
>
> He never did one thing wrong,
> Not once said anything amiss.
>
> They called him every name in the book and he said nothing back. He suffered in silence, content to let God set things right. He used his servant body to carry our sins to the Cross so we could be rid of sin, free to live the right way. His wounds became your healing. You were lost sheep with no idea who you were or where you were going. Now you're named and kept for good by the Shepherd of your souls. (1 Peter 2:21-25 MSG)

Through Jesus' death and resurrection, we possess the power to withstand the forces of all inner and outer rainbands in our lives!

PRAYER

Lord, I praise You for being my heavenly Father and disciplining me when needed. Thank You for Your correction that never gives me what I deserve, but is used to refine me. Please forgive me for my sins and help me to walk with You all the days of my life. I am so grateful my future is not defined by my past! I pray, Lord, that when I suffer because of the sins of others, I will handle the battering of outer rainbands like Jesus. I am confident You can take what was meant for evil against me and turn it into something good. Every hardship can be overcome through You and I will not be defeated! Thank You, Lord, for Your mercy, Your grace, and Your everlasting, unconditional love! In the name of Jesus, My Reedemer, I pray, Amen!

CHAPTER 11

STORM SHELTER
His Protection Even Through God-Sent Storms

But I will sing about your strength. I will rejoice in your love every morning. You have been my place of safety, the place I can run to when troubles come (Psalm 59:16 ERV).

Nature's storms vary from showers to thunderstorms, hailstorms, blizzards and other disasters. Likewise, there are life storms caused by satan, our own sin, the sins of others—and there are also times when the Lord Himself uses storms to work in our lives. We tend to draw nearer to God in the pouring rain than in the bright sunshine. Like the disciples who looked for and found Jesus whenever storms raged, we also grab onto Him when the waves overtake us.

Problems such as illness, divorce, death, and financial woes may cause us to question God's goodness and His plan at times, but it is through these same storms the Lord shows us: "My grace is all you need. Only when you are weak can everything be done completely by my power" (2 Corinthians 12:9 ERV).

Sometimes He allows us to get to the end of ourselves so we will start reaching out to Him. God uses storms to teach us to stop trying to do things in our own strength and to rely on His power instead. We cannot control the storms in our lives; we can only control our choice to either trust and follow the Lord or not. When we choose Christ we become victors instead of victims.

Our faith increases when we depend on Jesus. He alone can calm our raging seas and He is our shelter in the storm. "The LORD is my rock, my fortress, and my savior; my God is my rock, in whom I find protection. He is my shield, the power that saves me, and my place of safety" (Psalm 18:2).

But if we've never been in the midst of a storm, how do we know we can rely on the Lord to rescue us?

In 2004, Florida suffered four hurricanes in one season. My family survived Hurricane Charley with minimal damage, but then Hurricane Frances threatened landfall. As a single mother of three children, I didn't feel safe riding the storm out in our mobile home so we sought shelter at my mother's house in Tennessee. Our wait proved longer than we anticipated because it took over a week after the hurricane passed for power to be restored to our area. Storm-weary, we finally arrived home a few weeks later at 2:00 a.m. to find our screened enclosure completely gone. Only a scar of cement lay across the grass, marking where it had been.

Also in our absence, the state bird of Florida had completely taken over. Upon opening the doors to the van, we were engulfed in a cloud of vicious mosquitoes and had to bat them away as we made a mad dash to the house. Already feeling pretty beaten up, when I opened the front door we were smacked in the face by the most horrible smell. As I tried to assess the assault, my two girls crawled into their beds while my seven-year-old son bravely entered the kitchen with me, ready to do battle.

I opened the refrigerator and discovered what becomes of food when it has been closed in with no electricity for several weeks. The sight and smell had us both gagging over a wastebasket. I suddenly felt completely overwhelmed. After spending almost two weeks glued to the weather channel worried about what I would find (or not find) when I returned, and then driving thirteen hours with three children only to face all of this in the middle of the night took its toll. I wanted nothing more than to crawl into bed and pull the covers over my head. Since we had to breathe though, the food had to go—and now.

My trooper son held garbage bags open while I dumped armloads of rancid, unrecognizable products into them. Through my tears, I began noticing little white dots covering my arms. With growing horror I realized what they were—maggots!

I scrubbed the refrigerator until it was spotless, only it wouldn't stay that way. Maggots kept crawling out of the crevices. I would wipe every inch of it clean only to open the door later and find maggots everywhere again. They just continued appearing.

Since it was impossible to store food in the refrigerator and with no money to buy a new one, I pulled out an old cooler to keep a few of the most necessary items in, but we couldn't live like that for long. Even though the hurricane had passed, we were still in the midst of a raging storm and in desperate need of provision.

In despair, I cried out to my Father in prayer and a short time later I received a phone call from an acquaintance who had heard about our predicament. He knew someone who wanted to buy our refrigerator and take us to get a new one. While grateful, I didn't understand this reasoning at all. I explained again that maggots infested our refrigerator. If they had the money, why would these people want my nasty refrigerator instead of buying a new one for themselves?

As only the Lord can orchestrate, it turned out these folks were opening a bait shop and they wanted exactly what I had—a maggot-filled refrigerator! While their bait feasted on maggots, we enjoyed a sparkling clean, brand new refrigerator.

Hurricane Ivan was already on its way, but I now knew we could weather any storm with the Lord. My faith had increased, but I never would have understood the depth of God's care had I not been forced to endure this challenge.

The Lord allows trials at times to increase our faith and He also uses them to test our faith. Testing our faith is like working out. It increases our strength. The more we build up our faith, the more we can endure in the future. There will always be more storms, so the Lord in His mercy prepares us. Because I witnessed first-hand God's divine provision during the aftermath of Hurricane Frances, when Hurricane Ivan and Hurricane Jeanne hit, I didn't experience the same level of fear. I knew the Lord would be my shelter in the storm and I could agree with the Scripture: "And my God will meet all your needs according to the riches of his glory in Christ Jesus" (Philippians 4:19 NIV).

God tested Abraham's obedience and willingness to sacrifice everything for the Lord. He instructed Abraham to take his son to Mt. Moriah and sacrifice him to the Lord. Abraham did as he was told and the Lord honored his submission:

> So both Abraham and his son went together to that place. When they came to the place where God told them to go, Abraham built an altar. He care-

> fully laid the wood on the altar. Then he tied up his son Isaac and laid him on the altar on top of the wood. Then Abraham reached for his knife to kill his son.
>
> But the angel of the Lord stopped him. The angel called from heaven and said, "Abraham, Abraham!"
>
> Abraham answered, "Yes?"
>
> The angel said, "Don't kill your son or hurt him in any way. Now I can see that you do respect and obey God. I see that you are ready to kill your son, your only son, for me."
>
> Then Abraham noticed a ram whose horns were caught in a bush. So Abraham went and took the ram. He offered it, instead of his son, as a sacrifice to God. So Abraham gave that place a name, "The Lord Provides." Even today people say, "On the mountain of the Lord, *he will give us what we need.*" (Genesis 22:8-14 ERV, emphasis added)

Abraham prevailed through the most horrendous storm imaginable to a parent and he learned the Lord really does provide.

Likewise, after being tested in the wilderness, the Israelites were then able to rely on their memories of God's faithfulness to help them endure future trials:

> Remember how the Lord your God led you through the wilderness for these forty years, humbling you and testing you to prove your character, and to find out whether or not you would obey his commands. Yes, he humbled you by letting you go hungry and then feeding you with manna, a food

previously unknown to you and your ancestors. *He did it to teach you that people do not live by bread alone; rather, we live by every word that comes from the mouth of the Lord.* For all these forty years your clothes didn't wear out, and your feet didn't blister or swell. Think about it: *Just as a parent disciplines a child, the Lord your God disciplines you for your own good.* (Deuteronomy 8:2-5 emphasis added)

When we find ourselves in times of testing, it helps to remember the Lord's promise in James 1:12: "God blesses those who patiently endure testing and temptation. Afterward they will receive the crown of life that God has promised to those who love him."

Once we understand testing helps us to grow and we can trust the Lord to see us through it, our goal should be to say like Job: "And when he tests me, I will come out as pure as gold" (Job 23:10).

The Lord will allow trials to mold our character into being more like Christ. Trials that teach us humility, patience, kindness, love, discernment, trust, faith, steadfastness, and to "walk in a manner worthy of the Lord" (Colossians 1:10 NASB). God never tests us to be spiteful. His trials serve a divine purpose.

The Apostle Paul experienced great revelations from the Lord and a closeness with Him that could have caused Paul to boast. Instead, the Lord allowed Paul to be given a "thorn in the flesh" to keep him humble.

> So to keep me from becoming proud, I was given a thorn in my flesh, a messenger from Satan to torment me and keep me from becoming proud.
>
> Three different times I begged the Lord to take it away. Each time he said, "My grace is all you need. My power works best in weakness." (2 Cor. 12:7-9)

This was used to give Paul the grace to say: "So now I am glad to boast about my weaknesses, so that the power of Christ can work through me. That's why I take pleasure in my weaknesses, and in the insults, hardships, persecutions, and troubles that I suffer for Christ. For when I am weak, then I am strong" (12:9-10).

While some storms can be used to guard us from ourselves and train us to be more Christ-like, there are also ones to protect us from wrong situations. Have you ever enjoyed a sunny day only to be caught in a sudden shower? Taking shelter is not what you planned, but later on you find out if you hadn't gotten off that road you would have run head-on into an even bigger squall. Believe that the roadblock and alternate route have a purpose, and trust the journey you are on now.

Undoubtedly, there are occasions in all our lives when we're glad the Lord didn't answer a specific prayer the way we wanted Him to at the time! Proverbs 3:5-6 says: "Trust in the LORD with all your heart, and lean not on your own understanding; In all your ways acknowledge Him, and He shall direct your paths" (NKJV).

There may be times when you're doing everything right and even being zealous for the Lord through your involvement with church and ministry, but you still end up blindsided by a storm. Storms may develop to bring us back to our first love. God tells us:

> I know what you do, how you work hard and never give up. I know you do not put up with the false teachings of evil people. You have tested those who say they are apostles but really are not, and you found they are liars. You have patience and have suffered troubles for my name and have not given up. *But I have this against you: You have left the love you had in the beginning.* So remember where you

were before you fell. Change your hearts and do what you did at first. If you do not change, I will come to you and will take away your lampstand from its place. (Revelations 2:2-5, emphasis added)

Just as we desire our romantic relationships to stay on fire, the Lord wants us to burn with passion for Him. We often find ourselves in busy service for God, but at the sacrifice of spending quality time with Him. We forget the hunger we first had for His Word and we feed ourselves with works instead. The Lord wants our hearts more than our ministry. He says: "I'm after love that lasts, not more religion. I want you to know God, not go to more prayer meetings" (Hosea 6:6 MSG).

Jesus wants us to love Him with total abandonment—to put Him first above everything else in our lives. We have to dedicate time to our human relationships to keep them alive, and we must also devote ourselves to our First Love. When David sinned with Bathsheba he realized how far he had strayed from the Lord and he pleaded: "Restore to me the joy of your salvation" (Psalm 51:12). David hadn't lost his salvation, but he did lose the joy that comes with a close fellowship with the Lord.

Sometimes it takes a loved one to say they are leaving us before we realize how distant we've become. It forces us to refocus on our relationship. Likewise, a storm may need to happen for us to run back to Shelter. When the winds are whipping about and the power goes out, that's often the wake-up call for a deeper prayer life, worship, and a time of drawing closer to Him. Remember your passion when you first fell in love with the Lord and rekindle the sacred romance.

We are going to be hit by storms of all different magnitudes, but whatever their source is, we have the peace of knowing the

Lord is our shelter in the storm and will protect us through it all. He promises:

> The LORD guards you. The LORD is the shade that protects you from the sun. The sun cannot hurt you during the day, and the moon cannot hurt you at night. The LORD will protect you from all dangers; he will guard your life. The LORD will guard you as you come and go, both now and forever. (Psalm 121:5-8)

PRAYER

Merciful Father, let my mouth be filled with Your praise and with Your glory all the day.[1] Thank You for being a God full of compassion, and gracious, longsuffering and abundant in mercy and truth.[2] Please help me to rejoice in the storms knowing that through them I will develop endurance, strength, hope, and a stronger faith in You. I need You so I can persevere and do Your work. Teach me patience and guide me to be all that You want me to be. Help me to trust in Your ways and rely on Your plans. Thank You for leading my attention back to You and bringing me back to my First Love. I pray to always love You with total abandonment. I pray this in the precious name of Jesus, My Refuge from the Storm, Amen!

CHAPTER 12

RIDING THE STORM OUT
Drawing Closer to God

Draw near to God, and he will draw near to you (James 4:8).

When you are forced to ride out a storm, do you turn to worry or do you turn to God? The Bible tells us: "Don't worry about anything, but pray about everything. With thankful hearts offer up your prayers and requests to God. Then, because you belong to Christ Jesus, God will bless you with peace that no one can completely understand. And this peace will control the way you think and feel" (Philippians 4:6-7 CEV).

However, prayer is often used as a last resort. Worry won't change your situation, but God will.

We board our windows, stock our pantry with canned goods and water, prepare our generators, and fill our bathtubs, but we often neglect to prepare our spiritual dwelling. God is our source and strength and He is our shelter in the storm. Drawing closer to Him keeps us safe.

Above all, God desires a relationship with us. We were created for relationships—first with Him and then with others: "Then God said, 'Let us make human beings in our image, to be like us'" (Genesis 1:26); "Then the Lord God said, 'It is not good for the man to be alone. I will make a helper who is just right for him'" (Genesis 2:18).

The Lord interacted with Adam after He created the animals: "The Lord God used dust from the ground and made every animal in the fields and every bird in the air. He brought all these animals to the man, and the man gave them all a name."

He spent time with Adam and Eve in the Garden of Eden: "During the cool part of the day, the Lord God was walking in the garden" (Genesis 2:19 ERV).

We serve a relational God.

Unfortunately, the actions of Adam and Eve severed that intimacy. Their sins brought the storms of life and even though we will never be free from trials on this earth, our reactions and the outcomes of these storms are influenced by our closeness to the Lord.

While Adam and Eve ran *from* God, we should run *to* God. Nothing is secret from our All-Knowing God, and our response should be to confess our sins. Unconfessed sins keep us distant from our Savior. It leaves us out in the open, unprotected from the elements instead of in our Safe Haven.

Rather than hiding your sins, allow the Lord to be your Hiding Place. "Let us draw near to God with a sincere heart and with the full assurance that faith brings, having our hearts sprinkled to cleanse us from a guilty conscience and having our bodies washed with pure water" (Hebrews 10:22 NIV).

An intimate relationship with the Lord is to be our first priority. When asked what the greatest commandment is "Jesus replied,

'You must love the LORD your God with all your heart, all your soul, and all your mind'" (Matthew 22:37).

To love with all your being requires time and commitment. You must dedicate yourself fully to the task of ensuring loving relationships with your significant other, your family and your friends. Similarly, efforts have to be made towards developing a sacred romance with Jesus.

If you've been in love, you know the pleasure of spending time getting to know that person and growing closer together. When you love God, spending time with Him should also be a joy as you foster a burning desire to know Him even more. Cry out like the Psalmist did: "As the deer longs for streams of water, so I long for you, O God" (Psalm 42:1).

Seek to nurture a closer relationship with God through activities that draw you personally to Him. One of the ways I feel intimate with the Lord is by taking walks in nature. The breeze is like a caress, the colorful wildflowers a gift, and the singing birds are His music to me. It's hard to be in nature and not praise our Creator.

Spending time with God is important. We can lose the closeness and intimacy with a loved one when we don't devote ourselves to them, and we can also lose the feeling of nearness to the Lord.

Have you ever gone through trials in your life and felt like the Lord wasn't there? Even David, a man after God's own heart, felt distant from God at times. Many of the Psalms reflect those feelings. While sometimes the Lord may purposely remain silent, this detachment is often because we aren't spending enough time with Him. Many marriages end when couples experience a disconnect:

"We never talk."

"We hardly ever see each other."

"I don't know him anymore."

Communication is key. We communicate with God through praise and worship, reading the Bible, fellowshipping with other believers in Christ, following the Holy Spirit, allowing Jesus to be Lord of our lives, and praying.

A garden needs water and sun to grow, and in order for us to thrive as Christians, we need Living Water and the Son. We also must be rooted in the soil of His Word. Jesus makes Himself known through the Word of God and the more time we spend reading the Bible, the closer we become to Him. Since the Lord speaks through His written Word, understanding the Scriptures will help us to distinguish what God is saying to us. Hebrews 4:12 says: "What God has said isn't only alive and active! It is sharper than any double-edged sword. His word can cut through our spirits and souls and through our joints and marrow, until it discovers the desires and thoughts of our hearts" (CEV).

Everyone appreciates the love language of affirmation, and our relationships flourish through heartfelt communication. Expressions of love and gratitude draw you closer to your loved ones. In the same way, speak to yourself words of affirmation from the Lord and enter into His presence:

I am a son or daughter of the King: "I will be your father, and you will be my sons and daughters, says the Lord All-Powerful" (2 Corinthians 6:18 ERV).

I am special: "You made all the delicate, inner parts of my body and knit me together in my mother's womb. Thank you for making me so wonderfully complex! Your workmanship is marvelous—how well I know it" (Psalm 139:13-14).

I am redeemed: "He is so rich in kindness and grace that he purchased our freedom with the blood of his Son and forgave our sins" (Ephesians 1:7).

I am victorious: "For I can do everything through Christ, who gives me strength" (Philippians 4:13).

I am favored: "For whoever finds me finds life and receives favor from the Lord" (Proverbs 8:35).

I am blessed: "You are truly blessed! The Lord is with you" (Luke 1:28 CEV).

I am joyful: "I have told you these things so that you will be filled with my joy. Yes, your joy will overflow!" (John 15:11).

I am chosen: "You are mine" (Isaiah 43:1 ERV).

I am free: "So if the Son sets you free, you are truly free" (John 8:36).

I am worth dying for: "When we were utterly helpless, Christ came at just the right time and died for us sinners. Now, most people would not be willing to die for an upright person, though someone might perhaps be willing to die for a person who is especially good. But God showed his great love for us by sending Christ to die for us while we were still sinners" (Romans 5:6-8).

I am always on God's mind: "How precious are your thoughts about me, O God. They cannot be numbered! I can't even count them; they outnumber the grains of sand! And when I wake up you are still with me" (Psalm 139:17-18).

I am truly loved: "I have loved you with an everlasting love. I have drawn you with loving-kindness" (Jeremiah 31:3 NIV).

We grow closer to others when we feel loved by them. The Apostle Paul recognized this fact and that is why he prayed for us to draw closer to the Lord through the understanding of God's great love for us: "And I pray that you and all God's holy people will have the power to understand the greatness of Christ's love—how wide, how long, how high, and how deep that love is" (Ephesians 3:18 ERV).

Prayer is a way of communicating your deepest thoughts and requests to God. It's sharing your true, honest feelings with Him. It's not about being eloquent, it's about baring your soul. It's about speaking and listening. It's about loving and being loved.

Connecting with God through prayer is not about drawing attention to ourselves but drawing closer to Christ, and it is to be from our hearts. When asked about prayer, Jesus said:

> "And when you come before God, don't turn that into a theatrical production either. All these people making a regular show out of their prayers, hoping for stardom! Do you think God sits in a box seat?
>
> "Here's what I want you to do: Find a quiet, secluded place so you won't be tempted to role-play before God. Just be there as simply and honestly as you can manage. The focus will shift from you to God, and you will begin to sense his grace.
>
> "The world is full of so-called prayer warriors who are prayer-ignorant. They're full of formulas and programs and advice, peddling techniques for getting what you want from God. Don't fall for that nonsense. This is your Father you are dealing with, and he knows better than you what you need. With a God like this loving you, you can pray very simply. Like this:
>
> Our Father in heaven, may your name be kept holy. May your Kingdom come soon. May your will be done on earth, as it is in heaven. Give us today the food we need, and forgive us our sins, as we have forgiven those who sin against us. And don't

let us yield to temptation, but rescue us from the evil one. (Matthew 6:5-13)

When Jesus shared the Lord's Prayer He wasn't instructing us to follow a formula. God is more interested in our hearts than the pattern of words we use, and there is no precise method to prayer. Jesus simply gives us examples of things to include, such as: worship (Our Father in heaven); praise (may your name be kept holy); recognizing God's authority and being obedient to His will for our lives (May your Kingdom come soon. May your will be done on earth, as it is in heaven); bringing our requests to the Lord (Give us today the food we need); confession (forgive us our sins); forgiveness (as we have forgiven those who sin against us); victory over sin and His protection from the attacks of satan (And don't let us yield to temptation, but rescue us from the evil one).

Nehemiah, a cupbearer to the king, was a powerful prayer warrior. When he heard the walls of Jerusalem still lay in ruins, leaving the Jewish exiles without protection, he drew near to the Lord in prayer: "When I heard this, I sat down and wept. In fact, for days I mourned, fasted, and prayed to the God of heaven" (Nehemiah 1:4).

Then Nehemiah praised God: "O LORD, God of heaven, the great and awesome God who keeps his covenant of unfailing love with those who love him and obey his commands, listen to my prayer!" (1:5-6).

Nehemiah confessed his sins and reminded the Lord of His promises. Then he asked the Lord for favor: "Please grant me success today by making the king favorable to me. Put it into his heart to be kind to me" (1:11).

When the time came for Nehemiah to meet with the king, the king not only allowed Nehemiah to travel to Judah to rebuild the walls, but he also addressed letters to the governors granting safe passage and timber for the construction project, as well as sending along army officers and horsemen to protect Nehemiah. "The king granted these requests, *because the gracious hand of God was on me*" (2:8, emphasis added).

God didn't answer Nehemiah's prayer because of the length of his request, but because of the sincerity of his appeal and Nehemiah's full trust in "the great and awesome God."

While Nehemiah's rich prayer life includes the longest prayer recorded in the Bible (Nehemiah Chapter 9), he also prayed short "arrow" prayers and received the same blessings:

> The king asked, "Well, how can I help you?"
>
> *With a prayer to the God of heaven*, I replied, "If it please the king, and if you are pleased with me, your servant, send me to Judah to rebuild the city where my ancestors are buried." (Nehemiah 2:4-5 emphasis added)

Mid-conversation, Nehemiah prays quickly and silently to the Lord before answering the king. Arrow prayers are brief petitions we shoot up to God, sometimes in our head as Nehemiah did. They are "help me!" prayers in the middle of a crisis, and "thank You" devotions in times of gratitude to our Lord. They are "bless you" intercessory prayers, and on the spot silent prayers for guidance, like Nehemiah's.

The Apostle Peter prayed the shortest prayer in the Bible. After he jumped out of the boat and was walking towards Jesus on the water, the fierce wind and waves frightened him and he began to sink. "Save me, Lord!" he shouted (Matthew 14:30). Three short but effective words. Then "Jesus immediately reached out and grabbed him" (14:31).

Many others in the Bible received blessings from their short, heartfelt prayers. Jabez prayed: "'Oh, that you would bless me and expand my territory! Please be with me in all that I do, and keep me from all trouble and pain!' *And God granted him his request*" (1 Chronicles 4:9-10, emphasis added).

When Jesus asked the blind man what he wanted Jesus to do for him: "'My Rabbi,' the blind man said, '*I want to see!*' And Jesus said to him, 'Go, for your faith has healed you.' *Instantly the man could see*, and he followed Jesus down the road" (Mark 10:51-52, emphasis added).

My prayer before my baby's surgery consisted of only three words: "God, help us!" My words were heartfelt and laced with agony and the Lord answered. He comforted me not only with the words of Jeremiah 29:11, but I also felt Him assuring me that the medical diagnosis was not the report of the Lord.

Deciding to trust the One who has the final say, I forgot everything that had been spoken over my child. Instead, I clung to God's promises while I embraced motherhood with a passion. Samantha thrived and the only reminder of the tragic first weeks of her life, the enflamed scar and protruding valve, soon disappeared under hair that grew like grass sprouting up after a forest fire. Samantha's skills increased and surpassed other children her age. By twelve months she could speak 38 words and at eighteen months she knew her entire alphabet by sight! All her doctor could say was to "take it for the miracle it is." Instead of struggling with disabilities, Samantha turned out to be gifted!

Whether long or short, the effectiveness of your prayers is attributed to your relationship with God. Prayer should be so natural that it's a part of your everyday life. It's praying without thinking, and engaging with the Lord at all times. Through this act of communion, you are fulfilling the directive of the Apostle Paul: "Never stop praying" (1 Thessalonians 5:17).

The closer you are to the Lord, the closer you are to answered prayers. God wants a deep, loving relationship with us so much that when our sins separated us from Him, God sent His only Son so we could embrace God through the outstretched arms of Jesus on the cross.

> But God is rich in mercy, and he loved us very much. We were spiritually dead because of all we had done against him. But he gave us new life together with Christ. (You have been saved by God's grace.) Yes, at one time you were far away from God, but now in Christ Jesus, you are brought near to him. You are brought near to God through the blood sacrifice of Christ." (Ephesians 2:4-5, 13 ERV)

Ride the storm out by trusting God to bring you through it. The storm will end. At some point the wind and the rain will cease and the sun will shine again. "So whenever we are in need, we should come bravely before the throne of our merciful God. There we will be treated with undeserved kindness, and we will find help" (Hebrews 4:16 CEV).

Draw close to God. He is waiting with outstretched arms.

PRAYER

Heavenly Father, please fill me with a hunger for the things of God. "Lord, this is what I seek: that I may dwell in the house of the LORD all the days of my life, to gaze upon the beauty of the LORD and to seek Him in His temple."[1] Like Abraham, I want to walk with You, Lord, and be called a friend of God. Help me to declare: "For to me, to live is Christ and to die is gain."[2] Deepen my attachment to You. Thank You, Jesus, for coming and tearing the veil so I can be closer to God. Grow my faith, Lord, because "[w]ithout faith it is impossible to please Him, for he who draws near to God must believe that He is, and that He is a rewarder of those who seek Him.[3] Give me clean hands and a pure heart so I may ascend into the hills of the Lord and stand in Your holy place.[4] Let my heart become one with Yours. In the name of Jesus, My Friend, I pray, Amen!

CHAPTER 13

TRAVEL ALERT
Storms Don't Mean You're Out Of God's Will

The LORD says, "I will guide you along the best pathway for your life. I will advise you and watch over you" (Psalm 32:8).

It's a gorgeous day with the sun sparkling off the water like a million diamonds and a slight breeze caressing your skin. As you walk down a path sprinkled with brightly colored wildflowers, a chorus of chirping birds and katydids are music to your ears. What a great day to be alive! There is a spring in your step and a song in your heart. But as you round a bend in the trail, the sky starts to darken as thick, threatening clouds roll in. The choir of wildlife changes to the rumblings of thunder. The wind is now whipping against you as you struggle to move forward. In the dimming light everything looks different and you are sure you've lost your way. Just a short time earlier you'd stepped out, confident in your direction.

Now you falter under the pressure of the storm and question whether you are on the right path after all. You felt led to take this journey and you even checked the weather reports before you left. There were clear skies with no travel alerts. It should have been a pleasant trip, yet here you are facing the storm of the century. Maybe you missed a turn and are heading in the wrong direction.

As the rain stings your eyes you begin to believe you should have stayed home. God didn't really orchestrate this journey after all. You must have misunderstood. Surely if you were in His will you wouldn't be drenched.

Even though storms aren't pleasant, when you run smack dab into the middle of one it doesn't necessarily mean you are on the wrong road. Like a flashing caution light, Psalm 34:19 warns: "Many are the afflictions of the righteous."

You are never traveling blindly because God sees the road in both directions, from beginning to end, and sometimes His purpose is to take you directly through the storm. Fear not, because you are also never traveling by yourself.

Three faithful servants of the Lord, Shadrach, Meshach, and Abed-nego, were following God when they found themselves in the middle of Nebuchadnezzar's fiery furnace, flames crackling around them. When Nebuchadnezzar peered into the flames, though, he saw four men standing in the fire. The men did not face the flames alone—Jesus stood with them.

Despite faithfully following the Lord's path on his missionary journeys, the Apostle Paul suffered many afflictions along the way. In Acts 23:11, God specifically instructed Paul: "Take courage! As you have testified about me in Jerusalem, *so you must also testify in Rome*" (NIV, emphasis added). It was the Lord who led Paul to Rome, yet Paul still encountered a shipwreck along the way.

Sometimes our lives feel like a shipwreck in the midst of our calling, but perseverance is key. We must trust the omniscience of the Alpha and Omega. As the famous theologian, J.I. Packer puts it: "Sooner or later, God's guidance, which brings us out of darkness into light, will also bring us out of light into darkness. It is part of the way of the cross."

Whether the Lord is allowing these storms to build our character or to test our faith, it is comforting to know the Lord Himself said, "I make known the end from the beginning, from ancient times, what is still to come. I say, 'My purpose will stand, and I will do all that I please'" (Isaiah 46:10 NIV).

When we trust the Lord and seek to follow His plan, He is our shelter. Even though we may not always understand His route, we can rely on God to guide us through. But the devil wants us to cower in a cave or turn back from our mission when storms brew. He tries to make us believe we must have heard wrong and it was our own misguided thinking that is leading us to this place. After all, if it really was the Lord's plan then everything would be sunshine and roses instead of doubts and struggles.

However, after the disciples participated in the great miracle of feeding 5,000 people with only five loaves of bread and two fish, Jesus (who knows all and foresees what is coming) sent the disciples right into the middle of a storm:

> Immediately after this, Jesus insisted that his disciples get back into the boat and *cross to the other side of the lake*, while he sent the people home. After sending them home, he went up into the hills by himself to pray. Night fell while he was there alone.
>
> Meanwhile, the disciples were in trouble far away from land, for a strong wind had risen, and

they were fighting heavy waves. (Matthew 14:22-24, emphasis added)

It's easy to automatically assume if you run into trouble you must not be following God, but that's not necessarily the case. When the Israelites left Egypt they followed the Lord as a cloud by day and a pillar of fire by night. There's no doubt God was guiding them, but storms still inundated their journey.

Jesus is one with God, but He still endured hardships continually throughout His missionary time here on earth. When Jesus went to the desert to be tempted by the devil, it was actually the Spirit who led Him there. "Then Jesus was led by the Spirit into the wilderness to be tempted there by the devil" (Matthew 4:1).

Of everyone, Jesus followed the exact plans of God, yet Christ suffered more than anyone.

There are times, however, when the Lord will use a storm in your path as a giant detour sign. Maybe your plans aren't objectionable, but you charted your course without consulting the Lord first and are traveling under your own power. Or maybe you started in the right direction but took a wrong turn. A storm might be what's needed to reroute you onto an alternate road.

Thankfully, God makes our paths straight when we trust in Him. He is the Lord of our lives and our Redeemer, and He can set us on the right course.

The Lord gave the prophet Jeremiah a lesson on the sovereignty of God when He told Jeremiah to go to the potter's house to receive a message from the Lord:

> So I went down to the potter's house and saw him working with clay at the wheel. He was making a pot from clay. But there was something wrong with the pot. So the potter used that clay to make

Travel Alert

> another pot. With his hands he shaped the pot the way he wanted it to be.
>
> Then this message from the Lord came to me: "Family of Israel, you know that I can do the same thing with you. You are like the clay in the potter's hands, and I am the potter." (Jeremiah 18:3-6 ERV)

The Lord takes each of us and creates us in a unique way for a special purpose. That purpose is to travel with Him along the journey, and not set out on our own. The Lord warns us:

> What sorrow awaits those who argue with their Creator.
>
> Does a clay pot argue with its maker?
>
> Does the clay dispute with the one who shapes it, saying, 'Stop, you're doing it wrong!'
>
> Does the pot exclaim, 'How clumsy can you be?'
>
> ...
>
> I am the one who made the earth and created people to live on it.
>
> With my hands I stretched out the heavens.
>
> All the stars are at my command. (Isaiah 45:9, 12)

We will enjoy the trip and arrive safely at our destination when we remain pliable in the Potter's hands.

Like the Potter molds the clay, the storms in our lives shape us, and even when clay is broken down it can still be remolded into something beautiful.

Our goal is to allow our vessel to be used in a way that brings the most glory to our Creator.

Ask God to give you discernment, and if there's peace in your spirit despite the storms, continue down the path with confidence.

Even if the rains are blinding you for the moment, the Lord will be your guide. His Word promises: "If you wander from the right path, either to the right or to the left, you will hear a voice behind you saying, "You should go this way. Here is the right way" (Isaiah 30:21 ERV). Allow Scripture and the Holy Spirit inside you to be your map.

Sometimes the map may not take you in the direction you intended, though, so be open to changing course. The prophet Samuel traveled to Bethlehem after God told him to go and anoint a new king from the house of Jesse (1 Samuel 16). When Samuel saw the good looks and stature of the first son, Eliab, he thought surely Eliab would be the new king. But God guided Samuel away from Eliab and all the other six sons standing before him too. David, the youngest son who was in the fields tending to the sheep, turned out to be God's chosen one. If Samuel hadn't relied on discernment from the Holy Spirit and adhered to God's direction instead of his own perception, he would have anointed the wrong king!

Maybe you're afraid to follow a certain path because you think you aren't gifted enough to pursue such a dream. Our greatest accomplishments, however, will always be due to the Lord working in us. He likes to shine through our weaknesses. The apostles weren't preachers, they were lowly fisherman. Moses was educated in the ways of the Egyptians, but he felt inadequate as a speaker. Gideon was too fearful to lead an army, and King David, the forgotten son, was a lowly shepherd boy! It's not about our own abilities but the power of God within us. "With God's power working in us, he can do much, much more than anything we can ask or think of" (Ephesians 3:20 ERV).

The Lord did much more than I could ever have imagined when I was inspired to write a screenplay for a feature film. Once I completed *Steadfast*, my goal was to sell the script to a production company for them to film the movie. However, I sensed I was not to sell it but to produce the movie myself. While it seemed like an incredible feat, in an act of obedience I moved forward. Feeling the blessings of God on the project from the very beginning, we experienced His favor in ways that made the impossible possible.

The storm along the road for me was when, during the very first day on the set, I received a phone call from the police telling me that my daughter had experienced a seizure and an ambulance was transporting her to the hospital. Racing down the highway to join her, the movie suddenly seemed insignificant to me and I almost lost my desire to continue.

By the grace of God I persevered and the rest of filming was one of the most fun, exciting, challenging, and rewarding times of my life. I'm so glad I didn't turn back.

Be courageous and live your dreams too! Don't let the threat of storms or feelings of inadequacy hold you back. He equips those who dare to be obedient. You were created to live an extraordinary life! The Apostle Paul said, "Therefore I, a prisoner for serving the Lord, beg you to lead a life worthy of your calling, for you have been called by God" (Ephesians 4:1).

The prophet Jeremiah thought he was too young to be used by the Lord. But God encouraged Jeremiah not to listen to false travel alerts but to confidently go where God was sending him. The Lord told him:

> "I knew you before I formed you in your mother's womb. Before you were born I set you apart and appointed you as my prophet to the nations."
>
> O, Sovereign Lord," [Jeremiah] said, "I can't speak for you! I'm too young!"

The Lord replied, "Don't say, 'I'm too young,' for you must go wherever I send you and say whatever I tell you. And don't be afraid of the people, for I will be with you and will protect you." (Jeremiah 1:4-8, emphasis added)

When the Lord calls us to do something we don't have to wait for perfectly clear skies to venture out, and we needn't run back home at the first threat of a storm. If God gives us a purpose, He will also give us the ability to accomplish that purpose despite any foul weather. We shouldn't seek the weatherman, but instead trust in the protection of our Umbrella and move forward. Through the journey of walking by faith we will discover Jesus is Lord over all—even the storms.

PRAYER

Heavenly Father, thank You that no matter what the weather looks like, Your Word promises if I do what the Lord wants, He will make certain each step I take is sure. The Lord will hold my hand and if I stumble, I still won't fall.[1] If my eyes are fixed on You, I don't have to question every travel alert or run back home at the sighting of storm clouds. Please direct my footsteps according to Your Word and let no sin rule over me.[2] I pray You will equip me with all I need for doing Your will; that You will produce in me, through the power of Jesus Christ, every good thing that is pleasing to You. Help me to not stress out in my search for the perfect avenue, but give me peace in the knowledge that, while there is only one road leading to You, there is not only one option in life for me. Your wonderful plan is for me to spend eternity with You, and You care more about how I live than where I live. I can choose different paths as long as I walk with You, remain faithful, and seek to glorify You. Then I will always be living in Your purpose since You are able to work all things according to Your will. Please make me pliable in the Potter's hand and mold something beautiful with my life. In the name of Jesus, Lord of All, I pray, Amen!

CHAPTER 14

IN THE EYE OF THE STORM
Be Still and Wait on God

Let all that I am wait quietly before God, for my hope is in him. He alone is my rock and my salvation, my fortress where I will not be shaken (Psalm 62:5-6).

Living in Florida has taught me a lot about hurricanes, and I learned I don't like them. Whenever a hurricane advances, my eyes are glued to the Weather Channel. When storm tracking, the biggest concern is where the eye of the storm is headed because closest to the eye are the strongest winds. Yet the eye itself is the calmest part of the storm. Inside the eye the winds are peacefully light and the skies are often clear. In the midst of a hurricane, the eye is the stillest place to be.

Even in the eye of the storm, however, fierce eyewalls will always be raging around us. Storms are continuously forming on the horizon and we find our days varying between sun and pleasant weather, overcast, threatening skies, and raging storms.

Our center of stillness is found in Jesus—our Eye in the Storm.

When we are being tossed about like a ship on a stormy sea, our lifeboat is the promise of Jesus when He spoke "Peace! Be still!" to the stormy waves and they stopped.

The Lord comforts us with His words: "Be still and know that I am God." The two parts of this statement are (1) being still, and (2) knowing He is God.

Many of us struggle with being still. We languish during the times we feel we aren't getting anywhere, and we fret our lives are being wasted. The clock is ticking. But God has a time for His purpose, and often our biggest mistakes are made when we don't wait for Him.

Through our fleshly misconceptions we often operate as if the Lord needs our help. We get a godly idea then do everything humanly possible to make it happen. God doesn't need our help—He's God.

When it's truly a God-given idea we need His help instead, because we won't be able to do it on our own. He is the One who equips and empowers us to do what He's called us to do. His Word says, "For apart from Me, you can do nothing" (John 15:5).

It is important to live by God's time and not man's. Waiting time is never wasted time with the Lord.

The Apostle Paul's journeys proved to be highly effective in evangelizing, but he ended up spending much of his time in prison. While it might seem like those periods in jail were a waste of time when instead Paul could have been traveling extensively and sharing the gospel, the Lord used those seasons for Paul to write four of the books of the New Testament! The Lord can use our "down time" for His glory, too.

The Bible tells us those "who wait on the Lord shall renew their strength; they shall mount up with wings like eagles, they shall run and not be weary, they shall walk and not faint" (Isaiah 40:31 NKJV). Nevertheless, waiting can be excruciating, especially in the fast-paced culture we live in today. We aren't used to waiting. We have fast food, instant responses through texting and email, microwaves, drive-through everything, and online shopping. During the times when we struggle to "be still" and wait on God, we can gain encouragement from Bible characters such as Mary and Martha, Moses, Noah, Abraham, Moses, Joseph, Paul, and even Jesus.

Mary and Martha had to wait several days for Jesus to come to their aid when their brother was sick. During that interval their brother, Lazarus, died. By the time Jesus arrived, Lazarus had been in the grave for four days. Mary and Martha must have experienced deep anguish and anger during their period of waiting. Far from them, Jesus appeared to be ignoring their prayers.

Have you ever felt like your dreams had died while waiting on the Lord? Did your prayers seem to go unanswered during His deafening silence?

When Jesus showed up at His appointed time, however, He raised Lazarus from the dead and elevated everyone's faith in Christ. He used their time of waiting to reveal the glorious power of the Lord over death. The greater purpose of God was worked out through waiting. "But when Jesus heard about it he said, "Lazarus's sickness will not end in death. No, it happened for the glory of God so that the Son of God will receive glory from this" (John 11:4).

Moses waited forty years in a desert before being called into the ministry God purposed for him. During his time as a prince in Egypt, Moses thought he was fulfilling God's purpose to free the Jewish people when he killed an Egyptian who was oppressing them. Even though God's purpose *was* to free the Israelites, that wasn't God's timing or plan. Moses fled to the desert and for forty years he hid while he tended sheep. This once upon a time prince lived as a fugitive with no more thoughts of doing anything great for God. Survival replaced vision.

Despite failing to wait on the Lord, God didn't forget Moses. Instead He was preparing him. Although being prince of Egypt trained Moses in leadership skills, he was hot-tempered, impulsive, and unaccustomed to hardships. Moses also possessed too much confidence in himself and not enough reliance on God. Once Moses the shepherd proved faithful in caring for sheep, God used him to care for the people of Israel. Reliance on his own strength to fulfill God's calling grew into dependency and obedience to God.

The Lord uses our time of waiting to develop our character so we will then possess the traits needed to carry out His plan. He waits for us to prove faithful with the small things so He can entrust us with greater things.

My own character has needed to be tweaked over the years. I'm an A-type personality: "A" for action. If I come up with an idea or if something needs to be done, I immediately start trying to figure out how to do it even if it seems unattainable. Sometimes that can be a good thing: like when the doctor said my daughter would be mentally challenged and instead I treated her as if she was Einstein and found ways to mentally stimulate her. At other times, however, my attempts at instant action have created storms.

The problem with instantaneous action is there's often a lack of prayer, or when there is a quick prayer, time isn't spent waiting for an answer. We are then attempting things in our own strength instead of through the power of the Lord.

Accepting the wrong job; beginning (and sometimes ending) relationships too soon; attempting a business venture without prayer and a solid plan; a hasty email or phone call that shouldn't have been made. Anything we pursue without the blessings of God is a hurricane in the making.

Some disasters in my life can be attributed to times when I moved too fast and stepped in front of God. Even though many of those endeavors hadn't been biblically unsound, the Lord wants us to walk with Him, not run ahead of Him. Through plenty of bruised emotions, busted wallets, broken hearts and fences, I've learned to pray first, then plan. To pause a moment and wait for the wisdom of the Lord. I still sometimes catch myself rushing forward, but my batting average is much stronger now.

To enter the big leagues, we must rely on God. Nothing worthwhile is accomplished without Him. As C.S. Lewis noted: "God can't give us peace and happiness apart from Himself because there is no such thing."

It's essential to understand that waiting on God's timing, however, doesn't mean doing nothing. We are still to move forward and work hard at everyday life. Moses provided for his family and learned to be a good shepherd during his time in the desert. He wasn't stagnant but worked at gaining the wisdom and humility he would later need to lead God's people.

The Lord also developed Joseph's character during the waiting time when Joseph was a slave and a prisoner in Egypt after being betrayed and sold by his brothers. Whereas Joseph entered into slavery a spoiled young man, after seventeen long years Joseph had the patience and fortitude needed to become second-in-command over all of Egypt and to save his people from starvation. Though it seemed long, Joseph's waiting time was definitely not wasted time.

When waiting seems like it'll never end, think of Noah. He actually knew without a doubt that his purpose was God-appointed.

The Lord specifically told Noah His plan for destroying all living creatures on earth. He also promised to keep Noah and his family alive, and even gave Noah explicit instructions on how to build the boat. "So Noah did everything exactly as God had commanded him" (Genesis 6:22).

You may think that if you actually heard God's audible voice you would also faithfully do whatever He asks. But would you really work at it year after year while waiting for the vision to be fulfilled? Or would you decide it was never going to happen after all and give up?

Noah faithfully worked and waited over a hundred years for something he had never even seen before—rain. People surely must have ridiculed him as he built a massive ark, but Noah continued with his mission year after year. Noah remained steadfast and in due season he did receive salvation for his family, along with confirmation that God's Word is undeniably true. But he waited a very long time before experiencing the fulfillment of God's plan.

Abraham also heard the voice of God delivering a promise. God told Abraham he would be the father of many nations. After ten years of anticipating the arrival of the promised child, his wife, Sarai, grew tired of waiting. Apparently deciding God needed a little help from them, she offered her maidservant to Abraham to impregnate and Abraham obliged, which causing huge problems (read Genesis 16-21).

Many of us also falter during our waiting season. While well-meaning, our interference shows we lack the trust to believe God will do what He says He will. Our impatience diminishes our faith. Taking matters into our own hands often leads to all kinds of trouble, and even sin. Abraham eventually did learn to wait on God and was finally blessed by God's promise through the birth of Isaac.

The Lord wants to do the same for us when we put our trust in Him. "I wait for the Lord, my whole being waits, and in his word I put my hope" (Psalm 130:5 NIV).

After his conversion, the Apostle Paul spent three years preparing before stepping into his mission, and even Jesus didn't begin His ministry until age thirty. This should be an encouragement to those of us who fear too much time has passed for our aspirations to ever come true. God's timing is not our timing and it is never too late. "But do not forget this one thing, dear friends: With the Lord a day is like a thousand years, and a thousand years are like a day" (2 Peter 3:8 NIV).

But how can we "be still" and wait on God when we are impatient to get married, to start a new job or ministry, to buy a house, to move to a new town? Again, being still doesn't mean not moving. It means seeking God's clear guidance and direction, then stepping out in His power and not our own. Being still means trusting God.

Walking with the Lord doesn't mean waiting for Him to clear every bit of debris from our path before going forward. We are still responsible for doing our homework by using the wisdom He's given us and the resources available to research the decisions we are contemplating (our biggest resource being the Bible). The "be still" part comes when we stop to determine whether the Lord is truly providing an open/closed door or if our own desires are causing His voice to be muffled in the fog. When pondering our next step we must keep in mind that "we don't yet see things clearly. We're squinting in a fog, peering through a mist" (1 Corinthians 13:12 MSG).

One of the most difficult obstacles in any Christian's walk is determining the small, still voice of the Lord through the haze of our own voice and the howling wind of the enemy. To "know that

I am God" requires drawing closer to Him. Spending time reading the Bible and knowing His Word will keep you from mistaking another voice for His. Jesus said, "My sheep listen to my voice; I know them, and they follow me" (John 10:27).

Be still and know He is God by making prayer a priority; not only by speaking to God, but by learning to listen to Him as well. Only through tuning into the Holy Spirit will you be able to tune out the voice of satan. This may seem unnecessary when the weather is pleasant, but danger can exist in the eye of the storm if you become complacent. When the seas are calm, if you loosen the moorings even just a little, you face being hit by the destructive force of the eyewall that surrounds the edge of the eye.

It is often during our greatest times of peace when we let our guard down and risk being broadsided by satan. The devil is always seeking an opportune time to attack and he will try to tempt you to take shortcuts during your time of waiting. Stay moored to the Holy Spirit and pray like Solomon: "So give Your servant an understanding mind and a hearing heart…so that I may discern between good and evil" (1 Kings 3:9 AMP).

Satan cannot outsmart you when you are grounded in God's Word and familiar with his schemes.

In the waiting, the Lord will give you strength, guidance, hope, wisdom, provisions, and open doors (He will also sometimes close doors). Being still develops patience and humility. It transforms your character as other traits are tweaked to fit God's plan and purpose for you. Most importantly, being still draws you into a closer relationship with the Lord. And that is the best place to be.

"For since the world began, no ear has heard and no eye has seen a God like you, who works for those who wait for him!" (Isaiah 64:4).

PRAYER

My Lord, thank You for being my Eye in the Storm, a place where I can be still and safe when the storms rage around me. Help me to wait on You but to never become complacent. Don't allow me to use waiting as an excuse for not taking action when needed. Instead, let this be a time for drawing nearer to You. A time of opening my ears to hear, my heart to receive, and my mind and body to then act under Your direction. Fill me with patience, wisdom, guidance, and strength. Encourage me with the knowledge that in this season of waiting, You are preparing me for even greater things. In the name of Jesus, Alpha and Omega, I pray, Amen!

CHAPTER 15

BLIZZARDS
Time to Shovel the Driveway (Move!)

> *The* Lord *our God said to us in Horeb, 'You have stayed long enough at this mountain. Turn and take your journey, and go to the hill country of the Amorites....See, I have set the land before you. Go in and take possession..." (Deuteronomy 1:6-8 ESV).*

Frothy white snow swirls outside the window, the blustery wind gathering it into heaping mounds across the driveway and yard. Naked trees are clothed in robes of white, and glittering icicles drip down from the eaves. The sight is a lovely reprieve from the gale-force winds and whiteout that had obscured all views in the early morning blizzard.

Then you realize the only way out is to shovel the driveway.

There are times in life for action. Even though we're always to wait for God's wisdom and guidance, there are periods to be still and seasons to move. While most of us are more comfortable waiting for God to act before stepping out in any fashion, sometimes we just have to go and shovel the driveway whether we feel like it or not.

Sometimes we are required to move into our miracle—to act first *and then* the blessings will follow.

There may be instances when we think we're waiting on God but what we're actually doing is stalling in comfort. It's easier to walk the same path than to venture down a different trail where the potholes are unknown. While familiarity might seem like a safer route, it also comes with the risk of settling for less than God's best. At times we just have to step out in faith and *move!*

At Horeb, the Israelites became too comfortable on the mountain. The Lord had brought them out of bondage to lead them to the Promised Land but they were settling for less than God's best. The Lord told them they had stayed on the mountain long enough and He instructed them to move—to go and possess the land.

The Israelites passed through storms along the way and so will we, but God always has been and always will be our Umbrella. As long as we are under the Umbrella, we can have the confidence to move forward.

God also spurred Moses into action after Moses rescued the Israelites from Pharaoh. The vast Red Sea lay before them and the king and his army were advancing from behind. Terrified, they cried out to the Lord for help.

But Moses told the people, "Don't be afraid. *Just stand still* and watch the Lord rescue you today. The Egyptians you see today will never been seen again. The Lord himself will fight for you. Just stay calm" (Exodus 14:13-14, emphasis added).

Moses tried to calm the fears of the frightened Israelites by telling them to stand still and let God fight for them. But that is not what the Lord wanted them to do. Yes, the Lord would fight for them, but He needed them to move. This was not a time to be still but a moment for action.

> Then the LORD said to Moses, "Why are you crying out to me? *Tell the people to get moving!* Pick up your staff and raise your hand over the sea. Divide the water so the Israelites can walk through the middle of the sea on dry ground." (Exodus 14:15-16, emphasis added)

The people had to put their faith into action. Moses acted first (picked up his staff and raised his hand over the sea) and then the miracle followed (the waters parted).

Later, Moses was again tested to act. As the Israelites wandered in the wilderness, they camped at a place void of water. The people complained to Moses, demanding he give them water to drink or they would surely die.

> Then Moses cried out to the Lord, "What should I do with these people? They are ready to stone me!"
>
> The Lord said to Moses, "*Walk out in front of the people. Take your staff, the one you used when you struck the water of the Nile, and call some of the elders of Israel to join you.* I will stand before you on the rock at Mount Sinai. *Strike the rock, and water will come gushing out.* Then the people will be able to drink." So Moses struck the rock as he was told, and water gushed out as the elders looked on. (Exodus 17:4-6, emphasis added)

Could God have provided water without the act of Moses striking a rock? Certainly! But the Lord chose to strengthen their faith in Him and also in their spiritual leader, Moses, through the act of Moses moving forward and carrying out God's instructions.

Umbrella in the Storm

Not only does the Lord often wait to provide the blessing until after we have stepped out in faith, but He also proves He is in control by giving us what we need at the very instant we need it and not a moment sooner. He is Jehovah Nick of Time, but He is never too late.

The next generation of wandering Israelites faced the same tests of faith as those under Moses' leadership. The Jordan River stood between them and the Promised Land:

> The LORD told Joshua, "Today I will begin to make you a great leader in the eyes of all the Israelites. They will know that I am with you, just as I was with Moses. Give this command to the priests who carry the Ark of the Covenant: *'When you reach the banks of the Jordan River, take a few steps into the river and stop there.'*" (Joshua 3:7-8)

Joshua told the Israelites the Lord would show Himself strong to them through their obedience of moving forward in faith. The priests were to carry the Ark of the Covenant and "as soon as their feet touch the water, the flow of water will be cut off upstream and the river will stand up like a wall" (Joshua 3:13).

> So the people left their camp to cross the Jordan, and the priests who were carrying the Ark of the Covenant went ahead of them. It was the harvest season, and the Jordan was overflowing its banks. *But as soon as the feet of the priests who were carrying the Ark touched the water at the river's edge, the water above that point began backing up a great distance away....*(Joshua 3:14-16)

The whole nation of Israel crossed the Jordan River on dry ground. But first the priests had to step out in faith and get their feet wet. God could have parted the waters ahead of them, but He opted to act *after* they put their faith into action. Sometimes we have to get our feet wet in anticipation of our miracle too.

In our complacency we often take the wait approach because we assume if it's too hard, then it must not be what we're supposed to be doing. The Israelites could have decided to wait until summertime or fall when the waters receded, but they would have missed the miraculous blessings of the Lord. God works with what we give Him and it only takes one step of faith for Him to part the waters of an entire river and bless us with dry ground.

You may be afraid to take that leap of faith, fearful of the time in between your feet leaving the ground until they solidly touch down again. Maybe you lack confidence in your abilities and prefer the safety of a cave than the outside elements. Gideon shared those fears. A timid man, Gideon hesitated to make any decisions to move forward without complete assurance.

In Judges Chapter 6, Gideon was afraid of the enemy, the Midianites, and he hid underground in a winepress while he threshed the wheat. The angel of the Lord appeared to Gideon in his hiding place, told Gideon the Lord was with him and even called this trembling man a "mighty hero!"

> Then the Lord turned to him and said, *"Go with the strength you have, and rescue Israel from the Midianites. I am sending you!"*
>
> "But Lord," Gideon replied, "how can I rescue Israel? My clan is the weakest in the whole tribe of Manasseh, and I am the least in my entire family!"
>
> The Lord said to him, "I will be with you. And you will destroy the Midianites as if you were fighting against one man." (6:14-16, emphasis added)

Knowing the Lord was with him, Gideon gained the courage to move forward and the Lord used him to rescue Israel from their enemies, confirming what is written in 1 Corinthians 1:27: "But God chose the foolish things of this world to put the wise to shame. He chose the weak things of this world to put the powerful to shame" (CEV).

You can also confidently move forward in whatever God is calling you to do because the Lord is always with you, too. You don't have to wait until you're stronger, richer, or smarter. Move and then watch what the Lord does!

Joshua was given the same assurance. When the Lord called Joshua to lead the people after Moses, He said, "I've commanded you to be strong and brave. Don't ever be afraid or discouraged! I am the Lord your God, and I will be there to help you wherever you go" (Joshua 1:9 CEV).

After the miraculous crossing of the Jordan River, the Israelites encountered Jericho. The walled city of Jericho was the first place God told the Israelites to conquer as they entered into the Promised Land. Similar to the way Gideon and his army had defeated the Amikalites with trumpets, empty pitchers and torches, the Lord also gave Joshua the victory at Jericho in an unlikely manner.

Fortified by thick walls and gates surrounding its entirety, Jericho was impenetrable to any army and God's plan for victory made no human sense. The Lord told Joshua:

> "You and your fighting men should march around the town once a day for six days. Seven priests will walk ahead of the Ark, each carrying a ram's horn. On the seventh day you are to march around the town seven times, with the priests blowing the horns. When you hear the priests give one long

blast on the rams' horns, have all the people shout as loud as they can. Then the walls of the town will collapse, and the people can charge straight into the town." (Joshua 6:3-5)

Even though it seemed like an impossible battle strategy, Joshua didn't wait around for what he would consider a better plan. Joshua and the people moved forward and did as the Lord commanded. On the seventh day: "When the people heard the sound of the rams' horns, they shouted as loud as they could. Suddenly, the walls of Jericho collapsed, and the Israelites charged straight into the town and captured it" (Joshua 6:20).

The falling of walls after the shouts of people is certainly a God-created scenario. Since the victory clearly belonged to the Lord, why didn't He simply collapse the walls when the Israelites first approached the city of Jericho instead of instructing them to march around it for seven days?

Sometimes God requires us to move in order to build our character. Proceeding in a direction unclear to us causes us to trust God's ways and not our own. In turn, our faith is strengthened when we witness His power and His faithfulness. God had already promised Joshua the victory in 6:2: "But the LORD said to Joshua, "*I have given you Jericho*, its king, and all its strong warriors" (emphasis added). God's promise was fulfilled *after* the Israelites marched in obedience.

Our successes may require a prolonged period of marching, so keep moving! Even before the walls come tumbling down, be patient and boldly shout in anticipation of God's guarantee that the battle is already won!

On occasions I've marched boldly into the Lord's blessings. One such experience of moving by faith happened in my early twenties.

Traveling is a passion of mine. To me, it's the ultimate adventure. The idea of seeing the natural beauty of God's creation, the architecture He's inspired men to build, and the chance to connect with people from all different cultures excites me. Deciding to make travel a career, I enrolled in travel school and a year later became a travel agent. After taking a cruise, however, I gained a new goal: to work on a cruise ship. I loved the fresh salt air, the exotic ports, and most of all, the friendliness of the crew and passengers.

Back home, I began my mission in earnest. I started calling the different cruise companies to find out about their hiring process, and I was fortunate enough (I call it a "God thing") to speak to a representative from Carnival Cruise Lines. He kindly spoke to me at length and encouraged me to apply as a purser, which was an officer position. That advice in itself turned out to be a blessing because up to that point I had decided to apply to become part of the entertainment staff and teach dance—only I had no idea how to ballroom dance! I was determined enough to enroll at Arthur Murray Dance Studio to learn, but it'd be years before I could possibly be an instructor and I was ready to leave yesterday (I quit my lessons right after that phone conversation!).

Padding my resume with all my administrative experience, I began stuffing envelopes. Only the more I researched, the more I realized my resume would likely end up lost in a pile of the thousands of resumes cruise companies continually receive.

While standard practice would be to mail the resumes and wait for a response, I prayed and felt the urging of the Lord to "move." I strongly sensed Him leading me to take action and seek out my blessing.

Flying early one morning from Detroit to Miami, I arrived at the Port of Miami mid-afternoon with resume in hand and secured a pass to board the same ship the helpful Carnival manager was working on (this was before all the heightened security). The purser's office paged him and when he arrived at the front desk and learned of the measures I had taken to interview with him, he hired me on the spot. I became one of the first female officers to work on Carnival's cruise ships!

For eight months I sailed between Nassau, San Juan, and St. Thomas, working hard, playing hard, enjoying the tropical islands and meeting wonderful people. Then I took a job with American Hawaii Cruises where I voyaged around the Hawaiian Islands for several years. I learned to scuba dive, windsurf, waterski, and golf, rode bikes down Haleakala Crater, pet a nurse shark, hiked Diamond Head, ate poi at luaus, and swam under countless waterfalls. Also during that time I backpacked Europe for four months while on my breaks.

Working on cruise ships ranks as one of the greatest experiences of my life and I fully believe the opportunity presented itself because I trusted the Lord and stepped outside the box. Like Moses, Gideon, and Joshua, when directed by the Lord I didn't just stand there, but instead I moved into my destiny.

Are you playing it safe and waiting on God when He's already told you to get moving?

Move, even when the road seems impossible. If it's too hard for you to do in your own strength, then it must be a God plan! The Lord works strongest in situations we can't control ourselves, and when we forge ahead instead of holding back, we demonstrate our dependence and trust in Him.

So grab your shovel and push aside the snow. Put your faith into action and know God will move you past the next whiteout too.

Umbrella in the Storm

PRAYER

Lord, You are a God of action and I ask You to please motivate me when it is time for me to move, and keep me still when I am supposed to wait on You. Never let me be passive, but to always be actively seeking what You have planned for my life. Help me to have the courage to step into the waters *before* the blessings, knowing You are always true to Your Word. Let my actions activate Your promises. But please, Lord, never let me move ahead of You, out of Your timing or Your will. I pray my actions will always be in perfect synch with Your plan. I give You all the praise, all the honor, and all the glory. In the name of Jesus, the Way, the Truth and the Light, I pray, Amen!

CHAPTER 16

SEA OF STORMS
Anchored in Faith

We have this hope as an anchor for the soul, firm and secure (Hebrews 6:19 NIV).

It's a gorgeous day for a boat ride. The sparkling water winks and the refreshing breeze calls your name. Carefree, you glide out of the harbor. Soon your line is cast and you lean back with hands clasped behind your head and feet up on the cooler. The only sounds are the waves lapping against the boat and the cry of seagulls circling overhead. You relax in the perfectness of the day.

Until you glance up into the sky and notice thick, dark clouds rolling in.

The water turns murky and the now biting wind lacerates your skin. In the distance, a sheet of rain moves across the water like a giant shadow, looming closer by the second. You quickly start the engine and the boat speeds forward, only to sputter and stall. Out of gas and drifting, the rolling swells are dipping the vessel from side to side as you dangerously approach a group of jagged rocks ten feet high. Swiftly you drop the anchor and sigh with relief. Even though you are about to get drenched, at least the anchor will keep you from smashing into the cliffs.

When life is about to dash us against the rocks, being securely fastened to Jesus as our anchor prevents us from blowing off course. Faith is the chain connecting us to the Anchor, joining us to God and giving us salvation and eternal life. We are attached to the Lord because of our belief in Him: the belief that we were created by a Holy God who sent His only Son to live a sinless life on earth before being crucified as the penalty for our sins; that through His selfless act He became guilty so we could become innocent; that Jesus is alive, reigning with the Father and interceding on our behalf, and we as believers will one day join them.

By faith we are victorious through Jesus over sin, satan, and death! "Who is it that overcomes the world? Only the one who believes that Jesus is the Son of God" (1 John 5:5 NIV).

Paul said in Ephesians 1:18-20:
> I pray that God will open your minds to see his truth. Then you will know the hope that he has chosen us to have. You will know that the blessings God has promised his holy people are rich and glorious. And you will know that God's power is very great for us who believe. It is the same as the mighty power he used to raise Christ from death and put him at his right side in the heavenly places. (ERV)

Faith is trusting God even when you don't understand. As Christian author Philip Yancy puts it: "Faith means believing in advance what will only make sense in reverse."

Hebrews Chapter 11 is often called the "Hall of Faith" because it lists many who walked by faith and trusted in the Lord's providence even when it didn't make sense. The word "faith" is listed twenty-four times in that chapter alone, and the phrase "by faith" nineteen times. Here are a few examples of faith noted in the Bible: By faith Noah spent over a hundred years constructing an ark; by faith Abraham left all that he knew and went to a land he knew nothing about; and by faith Moses chose a desert over the palace.

Living a life of faith means letting God be God and trusting He knows what He is doing. It is looking beyond our circumstances and focusing on Christ, choosing to believe He will make a way even when there seems to be no way. Psalm 112 gives us this confidence: "Surely the righteous will never be shaken; they will be remembered forever. They will have no fear of bad news; their hearts are steadfast, trusting in the Lord" (6-7 NIV).

However, walking through the hall of faith doesn't necessarily lead to a way out of trials and tribulation. Some of the faithful were rewarded *for* their faith while others suffered greatly *because* of their faith. While Enoch was spared death, Abel died for his faith. Many never received the full fruit of God's promises in their life on earth, but all of them still stepped forth in obedience and trusted in their eternal rewards.

How we walk is important because we don't win the marathon by owning the proper shoes. We cross the finish line into the Kingdom of God through repentance and faith. Jesus highlights this point in the Parable of the Two Sons:

> "But what do you think about this? A man with two sons told the older boy, 'Son, go out and work in the vineyard today.' The son answered, 'No, I won't go,' but later he changed his mind and went anyway. Then the father told the other son, 'You go,' and he said, 'Yes, sir, I will.' But he didn't go.

"Which of the two obeyed his father?"

They replied, "The first."

Then Jesus explained his meaning: "I tell you the truth, corrupt tax collectors and prostitutes will get into the Kingdom of God before you do. For John the Baptist came and showed you the right way to live, but you didn't believe him, while tax collectors and prostitutes did. And even when you saw this happening, you refused to believe him and repent of your sins." (Matthew 21:28-32)

Don't be fooled into practicing proper form without actually possessing a heart of faith. Actions speak louder than words. We are not to give lip service to the Word of God, but to act under the authority and respect of Christ. Thankfully this parable shows us that it doesn't matter where we start in the race. As long as somewhere down the path we grab tightly to the baton of atonement and run the race of faith, we'll cross the finish line into His Kingdom.

God loves us right where we are and faith takes us to where we need to be.

"For we walk by faith, not by sight" (2 Corinthians 5:7 NKJV) means we are to trust God no matter what our circumstances might look like. It's being assured He is God and nothing can happen outside of His plan.

Many people find this to be one of the hardest principles of the Christian life.

Had I been given an ultrasound later in my pregnancy the doctors most likely would have advised me to abort my baby (which I never would have), and when I look back to the very beginning of Samantha's life it scares me to think what might have happened if the Lord hadn't been controlling the storm.

Samantha came into this world and true to His Word, God took this little girl and used her for His glory. At the age of seven when we went on our first family mission trip together, there in a nursing home an elderly gentleman ambled over to me with tears streaming down his face. Holding the hand of my precious child he told me she had done something no one else had been able to do his entire life. Samantha introduced him to the Savior and prayed the salvation prayer with him.

Samantha continued to be mission-minded. In our hometown, she saw a homeless man on the streets carrying all of his belongings in plastic bags. Immediately Samantha engaged her little sister and brother and together they determined our new ministry would be to give backpacks filled with tarps, rain ponchos, toiletries, snacks, and Bibles to the homeless. We created Backpacks 'n Blessings and actively worked with the homeless for many years. Channel 6 and Channel 13 News interviewed Samantha when we handed out over 600 backpacks to the homeless in Daytona Beach, Florida one Christmas. Through her efforts to help the homeless, Samantha won the grand prize in the worldwide Focus on the Family "Make it Matter" contest. (You can watch the television interviews at www.barbarashoner.com/videochan6.htm. The newspaper and magazine articles are included at the end of this book.)

After enjoying dinner with the talented, Grammy winning artist, Natalie Grant, I watched Samantha stand onstage next to Natalie Grant at a concert in Baltimore and share with others her passion to help those less fortunate. With tears of gratitude, I once again thanked the Lord for keeping His promise to me in that hospital room. The Lord is ever faithful!

Hebrews 11:1 says: "Now faith is confidence in what we hope for and assurance about what we do not see" (NIV). Faith is relying on God's faithfulness. The Gospel of Matthew tells the story of a Roman soldier who fully trusted the Word of God:

> When Jesus returned to Capernaum, a Roman officer came and pleaded with him, "Lord, my young servant lies in bed, paralyzed and in terrible pain."
>
> Jesus said, "I will come and heal him."
>
> But the officer said, "Lord, I am not worthy to have you come into my home. *Just say the word from where you are, and my servant will be healed.* I know this because I am under the authority of my superior officers, and I have authority over my soldiers. I only need to say, 'Go,' and they go, or 'Come,' and they come. And if I say to my slaves, 'Do this,' they do it."
>
> When Jesus heard this, he was amazed. Turning to those who were following him, he said, "*I tell you the truth, I haven't seen faith like this in all Israel!* (8:5-10, emphasis added)

The Roman officer respected the authority of Christ and trusted His word.

"Then Jesus said to the Roman officer, 'Go back home. *Because you believed, it has happened.*' And the young servant was healed that same hour" (Matthew 8:13, emphasis added).

Faith is trusting God's Word for answered prayer before it even happens because if we receive our answer first, then it negates the need to believe.

When Jesus arrived at the tomb of Lazarus, Martha did not want Jesus to enter because Lazarus had been dead for four days. Jesus said to her: "Didn't I tell you that you would see God's glory if you believe?" (John 11:40). After Martha put her faith in Jesus, her prayers were answered and her brother lived.

Trust God to change the impossible into possible! Believe in your heart and spirit, and not in what you see or feel. While the world tells us, "Seeing is believing," God says, "Believing is seeing."

Strive to have the faith of Abraham who was obedient to God without actually seeing, instead of operating in the faith of Thomas who first had to see and touch the scars of Jesus before he would believe.

1 Peter assures us this type of faith will not be in vain: "You love him even though you have never seen him. Though you do not see him now, you trust him; and you rejoice with a glorious, inexpressible joy. The reward for trusting him will be the salvation of your souls" (1:8-9).

Joshua and Caleb believed in the faithfulness of God rather than the reality of the circumstances. As two of twelve spies sent to scout out the Promised Land, Joshua and Caleb looked beyond the fortified cities and powerful enemies and focused instead on a land flowing with milk and honey. Everyone else lacked faith and feared the giants:

> They [Joshua and Caleb] said to all the people of Israel, "The land we traveled through and explored is a wonderful land! And if the Lord is pleased with us, he will bring us safely into that land and give it to us. It is a rich land flowing with milk and honey. Do not rebel against the Lord, and don't be afraid of the people of the land. They are only helpless prey to us! They have no protection, but the Lord is with us! Don't be afraid of them!" (Numbers 14:7-9)

The people still believed it was impossible to possess the land and the Lord punished the Israelites lack of faith by not allowing them to enter the Promised Land. Only Joshua and Caleb received that honor.

Do you ever find yourself relating more to the faithless Israelites than the faithful duo? Are you focused more on your circumstances and fear sometimes you just don't have enough faith? The father of a demon-possessed boy felt the same way. He brought his son to be healed and Jesus asked to see the boy. When the evil spirit saw Jesus it caused the boy to convulse and foam at the mouth. The father told Jesus this had been happening to his son since he was a young boy:

> "The spirit often throws him into the fire or into water, trying to kill him. Have mercy on us and help us, if you can."
>
> "What do you mean, 'If I can?'" Jesus asked. "Anything is possible if a person believes."
>
> The father instantly cried out, "I do believe, *but help me overcome my unbelief!*" (Mark 9:22-24, emphasis added). Sometimes we don't necessarily struggle to believe in Christ, but we might question life's outcomes. We have faith in the power of God but doubt we'll really get the job we're seeking, the bills will get paid, or we'll receive our healing. The boy's father understood that without the help of God he could never believe as he ought to.

How can we increase our faith and remove doubt? Like the boy's father did, *ask*. Matthew 7:7 says: "Ask, and it will be given to you; seek and you will find; knock and the door will be opened to you" (NIV). The Lord says He diligently rewards those who seek Him.

Draw closer to the Lord through prayer. Worship Him. Spend time hearing and studying the Word of God. "So then faith comes by hearing, and hearing by the word of God" (Romans 10:17 NKJV).

Be confident that God is greater than any of us, His plan is better, and He promises to be with us always. "God's way is perfect. All the Lord's promises prove true. He is a shield for all who look to him for protection" (Psalm 18:30). Rely on God's Word, which never changes. "The grass withers and the flowers fade, but the word of our God stands forever" (Isaiah 40:8).

Faith is trusting the Word of God. The chain between the Anchor and you is strengthened when you believe what God says no matter how you feel or what you are facing. When you are under attack remember: "Yes, and the Lord will deliver me from every evil attack and will bring me safely into his heavenly Kingdom" (2 Timothy 4:18).

When you wonder how the bills will get paid, read God's Word in Deuteronomy and believe you will be blessed if you obey the Lord: "The Lord will make your businesses and your farms successful…You will have plenty of bread to eat. The Lord will make you successful in your daily work" (28:3, 5-6 CEV).

When you feel unloved, trust God loves you: "For the Lord your God is living among you. He is a mighty savior. He will take delight in you with gladness. With his love, he will calm all your fears. He will rejoice over you with joyful songs" (Zephaniah 3:17).

When you are lonely: "The eternal God is your refuge, and underneath are the everlasting arms" (Deuteronomy 33:27 NKJV).

And when you are fearful: "Don't be afraid. I saved you. I named you. You are mine" (Isaiah 43:1 ERV).

Keep securely fastened to the Anchor through your faith in God's Word. Instead of rolling over with the boat under the breaking waves, trust as the Psalmist did: "I cried out, 'I am slipping!' but your unfailing love, O Lord, supported me. When doubts filled my mind, your comfort gave me renewed hope and cheer" (Psalm 94:18-19).

Anchoring yourself to Christ will save you from being shipwrecked in the storms of life. Hallelujah!

"Know therefore that the Lord your God is God; he is the faithful God, keeping his covenant of love to a thousand generations of those who love him and keep his commandments" (Deuteronomy 7:9 NIV).

PRAYER

Lord, the Anchor of my soul, I pray to always remain securely fastened to You. When the waves of adversity threaten to knock me over, keep me from being shipwrecked. Please hold tight to me and don't allow me to drift off course. Let no storm from the enemy sever the chain of hope I cling to. Bind me to You, and help me to stay faithful as You are always faithful. I thank You for the peace I can have no matter the size of the waves, the strength of the wind, or the amount of rain because You are my Anchor in the storm. In the name of Jesus, Author and Perfecter of our Faith, I pray, Amen!

CHAPTER 17

FLOOD OF GRACE
God's Grace Washes Over You

The LORD rules over the floodwaters. The LORD reigns as king forever. The LORD give his people strength. The LORD blesses them with peace (Psalm 29:10-11).

When the floodwaters from Hurricane Harvey wreaked havoc in Houston, people formed human chains, saving adults, children, and even pets from flooded homes and rooftops.

In between the countless recollections of inspiring rescues is a tragic story of sacrificial love. One mother and her three-year-old child were swept into the floodwaters and floated down a canal, the daughter clinging to her mom. When the two were finally spotted and rescued, the mother was unresponsive while the daughter suffered from hypothermia but lived.

"The 41-year-old mother 'absolutely saved the child's life,'" Officer Carol Riley, a spokeswoman for the Beaumont Police Department, told *People*.

"They were in the water for quite some time," Riley says. "When the baby was found the baby was clinging to her. The mother did the best she could to keep her child up over the water."[1]

The grace of God is our protection too. We cling to Him and He keeps our heads above water. He never leaves us nor forsakes us, and He proved that by dying so we could live. "For the grace of God has appeared that offers salvation to all people" (Titus 2:11 NIV).

Jesus is the absolute love and blessing of God given to us as a gift. "God saved you by his grace when you believed. And you can't take credit for this; it is a gift from God" (Ephesians 2:8).

Writer and theologian Frank Buechner describes the grace of God this way:

> The grace of God means something like: "Here is your life. You might never have been, but you are, because the party wouldn't have been complete without you. Here is the world. Beautiful and terrible things will happen. Don't be afraid. I am with you. Nothing can ever separate us. It's for you I created the universe. I love you."
>
> There's only one catch. Like any other gift, the gift of grace can be yours only if you'll reach out and take it.
>
> Maybe being able to reach out and take it is a gift too.[2]

Grace is a gift; it is favor we don't deserve. Grace is usually coupled with mercy and the two often walk hand in hand. It is through God's mercy we are spared from the penalty we all deserve. While our sins scream punishment, the Lord chooses to bless us instead. That's God's grace.

At the age of fifteen I experienced the mercy and grace of God in a life-saving way. Standing on the side of a busy Michigan highway with a backpack over my shoulders and my thumb in the air, I waited for one of the cars whizzing by to pull over and take me closer to my high school crush in California. Even though I had given my heart to Jesus when I was eight, right now my heart yearned for my boyfriend who, against both of our wills, had recently moved across the country with his family. Not willing to spend summer break merely talking on the phone through the wee hours of the night, I told my parents I was vacationing with a girlfriend and her family in Upper Michigan—and headed down the road in the opposite direction.

Clouds of dust burned my eyes and throat as a giant eighteen-wheeler pulled off onto the shoulder. Jogging up to the cab, I wrestled to climb up and get in. Initially I pictured riding in the backseat of a four-door, sitting between fighting siblings and playing the license plate game. So when the lone, nondescript trucker with dark hair and beard told me he could take me all the way to Oklahoma, I excitedly settled in.

Naive, invincible, and in love, I had no geographical sense of the distance I needed to travel. As stars replaced the sun and darkness enveloped the cab, I balled up my sweatshirt and placed it against the window. Resting my head on it, I began to doze off. The trucker and I had only spoken briefly when I first accepted his ride, which included my lying to him by saying I was sixteen instead of fifteen. At the time I felt the need to seem older.

After hours of total silence except for the thumping of the tires on the pavement and the occasional whistling of wind when he cracked the window, my eyes grew heavy. I had just dozed off when the sound of gravel jolted me awake as the truck pulled over onto the shoulder and stopped. The man's menacing voice cut through my grogginess.

"When I was younger, my girlfriend hitchhiked and was raped and murdered." Hatred burned in his eyes as he scooted across the seat towards me. "She was sixteen just like you. Now I'm going to rape and murder you!"

Instinctively I reached for the door handle and pulled. Forgetting how high up the cab was, I hit the ground with a thud. Scrambling to my feet, I sprinted down the road, running in the middle of the lane and praying to draw attention. Lungs bursting, heart pounding, and legs shaking I ran as fast as I could, my mind not fully grasping the situation.

Suddenly rocks pierced my legs and embedded into my palms as I was tackled from behind. The trucker gathered me up and flipped me over his shoulder. Bouncing against him as he ran back to the truck, I noticed the road was completely deserted. No headlights even in the distance. Fear almost knocked me out with the realization that no one was near to save me.

Throwing me into the bed in back, he pinned down my flailing arms and legs. "I'm not really sixteen," I shouted. "I'm only fifteen!" As if that would make a difference.

"Truckers pull off the road and sleep all the time, so no one's going to be suspicious of my truck being parked here. Nobody's going to help you."

Defeat threatened to overtake me until I remembered I wasn't alone with this madman after all. "Jesus, help me!" I started screaming, over and over again.

Sitting on top of me, the trucker struggled to unbuckle his belt as I thrashed around, calling out to Jesus with every breath. "Stop saying that!" he yelled, slapping me in the face.

But I knew Jesus was the only one who could save me, and if He didn't, I would still rather die with His name on my lips than to be silent. Like a broken record, I screamed for my Savior.

While I found comfort in the name of the Lord, it only agitated my would-be killer. He took off his belt and wrapped it around my neck. "I told you to stop saying that! Stop already!"

The belt tightened around my neck and my cries became garbled. Right when I was about to pass out, the belt suddenly loosened and my assailant jumped back. With a look of surprise he climbed into the driver's seat and turned the key. I scrambled to compose myself.

It was like the holy hand of God had reached down and snatched him off me.

He drove to the next exit, pulled into a gas station and dropped me off. Picking up my backpack that he had tossed onto the ground, I hugged it to me. In shock, I felt God's grace washing over me like a tidal wave. Even though I had lied and been doing something I shouldn't have, the Lord supernaturally saved me that night. The man never got farther than taking off his belt. God's unconditional love had protected me. The mercy and grace of the Lord answered my cries.

I never did make it to California, and shortly afterwards my puppy love waned. My experience, however, led me to find true love in the Savior. I learned He really does hear us. The words of Hebrews 4:16 became alive to me: "So let us come boldly to the throne of our gracious God. There we will receive his mercy, and we will find grace to help us when we need it most."

I found comfort and healing in Romans 8:37-39, truly discovering that "overwhelming victory is ours through Christ, who loved us. And I am convinced that nothing can ever separate us from God's love. Neither death nor life, neither angels nor demons, neither our fears for today nor our worries about tomorrow—not even the powers of hell can separate us from God's love. No power in the sky above or in the earth below—indeed, nothing in all creation will ever be able to separate us from the love of God that is revealed in Christ Jesus our Lord."

I'm not promoting a belief that one can do something wrong and the Lord will automatically step in and fix everything. I don't know why the Lord chose to save me that night and I don't take it for granted. All I can say is, praise the Lord!

There's a woman in the Bible who also experienced unmerited favor after being caught in the act of adultery. When Jesus was teaching at the Temple in the Mount of Olives, a group of Pharisees dragged the woman before Him. They asked Jesus if they should stone her in accordance with the Law of Moses.

As the woman trembled before her accusers Jesus bent down and silently started writing in the dirt. While Jesus' finger moved through the dirt, the Pharisees kept demanding an answer, so Jesus stood up and said, "'All right, but let the first one who has never sinned throw the first stone!' Then he stooped down again and wrote in the dust" (John 8:7).

The words Jesus wrote remain a mystery. Was it a record of their sins or a list of their names? Was it a symbolic act or was He doodling to give them time to think about their actions? Whatever Jesus scrolled in the sand struck a cord and they all unclenched their fists and released their anger as stones plopped to the ground:

> When the accusers heard this, they slipped away one by one, beginning with the oldest, until only Jesus was left in the middle of the crowd with the woman. Then Jesus stood up again and said to

the woman, "Where are your accusers? Didn't even one of them condemn you?"

"No, Lord," she said.

And Jesus said, "Neither do I. Go and sin no more." (John 8:9-11)

Grace saved her and it rescues you and me. Even when we make a mess of our lives, God in His grace still loves us. We are His children. He leaves the ninety-nine sheep to come searching for the one who wandered off.[3] He drapes the finest robes over the prodigal son who squandered his inheritance on immoral living.[4] He forever stays loyal to the prostitute[5] and forgives scheming brothers.[6]

Two powerful words in the Bible are "but God." Used time and again, they are contrasting words that take the defeats in our lives and turn them into victories. When you are discouraged, be encouraged by knowing a "but God" is working in your life. Allow "but God" moments in the Bible to inspire you (emphasis added to the following):

"*But God* remembered Noah and all the wild animals and livestock with him in the boat. He sent a wind to blow across the earth, and the floodwaters began to recede" (Genesis 8:1).

"You intended to harm me, *but God* intended it for good to accomplish what is now being done, the saving of many lives" (Genesis 50:20 NIV).

"My health may fail, and my spirit may grow weak, *but God* remains the strength of my heart; he is mine forever" (Psalm 73:26).

"*But God* showed his great love for us by sending Christ to die for us while we were still sinners" (Romans 5:8).

"For the wages of sin is death, *but* the free gift of *God* is eternal life through Christ Jesus our Lord"(Romans 6:23).

"Jesus looked at them and said, 'With man this is impossible, *but* with *God* all things are possible'" (Matthew 19:26 NIV).

"But God" highlights the grace of God. Impossible situations turn possible. When you feel like nothing will ever change, know the words "but God" can change everything.

"*But God* is so rich in mercy, and he loved us so much, that even though we were dead because of our sins, he gave us life when he raised Christ from the dead. (It is only by God's grace that you have been saved!)" (Ephesians 2:4-5 emphasis added).

God's grace truly is amazing!

PRAYER

Lord, please flood me with Your grace. Thank You, Jesus, for through Your grace I can live an abundant life because You assure me: "And God is able to make all grace abound toward you, that you, always having all sufficiency in all things, may have an abundance for every good work."[7] Thank You for the salvation that is given to me through Your grace when I accept the gift. I praise You, Jesus, for graciously choosing me. If not for "but God" moments, I would be lost. Free and undeserved, Your mercy and grace wash over me and intervene on my behalf time and time again. Thankfully Your blessings don't depend on me. As Paul said, "yet not I, but the grace of God which was with me."[8] Your grace is so far beyond my comprehension that all I can do is praise You, Lord. Help me to always remember Your loving mercy and grace. This I pray in the gracious name of Jesus, my Savior, Amen!

CHAPTER 18

DANCING IN THE RAIN
The Power of Praise

Your unfailing love is better than life itself; how I praise you! I will praise you as long as I live, lifting up my hands to you in prayer (Psalm 63:3-4).

Backing out of the driveway, you struggle to see over the suitcases, beach towels and inner tubes piled against the back window. After a year of waiting, your lake vacation is finally here!

Halfway to your destination, however, raindrops begin pelting the windows. The sky darkens and you reach over to turn on the headlights. Like the thundercloud above, your children's tempers burst forth. The chaos inside echoes the fury of nature outside, while the monotonous slap of the windshield wipers are like a metronome. Doom and gloom (and a massive headache) dampen the drive.

Day two finds you with your face pressed against the cabin window, your tears mirroring the path of the raindrops. Instead of joyous shrieks from splashing in the lake, there is the relentless annoying screams of children being cooped up for too long together. Even your spouse's voice has taken on an irritating tone. And the weather forecast is predicting rain for the rest of the week. Definitely not the vacation you imagined!

After all the time spent collecting change in the money jar, you expected a sunny vacation and lasting memories. Storms never factored in. Yet here you are and you have a choice. Either you make a bad situation worse or you make the best of it.

Dust off the board games and shuffle the cards. Make a joyful noise singing songs. Play charades. While these might not be the activities you were intending, they could turn out to be some of your fondest memories.

Instead of staring dismally at the drizzle, run outside and dance in the rain! Squishing mud between your toes could be the therapy you need. "Life isn't about waiting for the storm to pass…It's about learning to dance in the rain" (Vivian Greene).

Since storms are inevitable and often hit when least expected, our happiness and joy is directly affected by our attitude. The Lord tells us to not let our hearts be troubled. We have a choice to praise the Lord during trials and trust He's in control, or we can miserably wallow in self-pity and give the devil a victory. When we choose to praise Him through the storm, our eyes are lifted above the clouds to our Savior. Our focus shifts from our problems to our Solution.

When we praise God, we are glorifying our Lord. We are thanking Him for His goodness in our lives. It is an expression of worship as we exalt the King of Kings. Praise demonstrates our faith and our trust that the Lord is ultimately in control of every situation. "The LORD is my strength and shield. I trust him with all my heart. He helps me, and my heart is filled with joy. I burst out in songs of thanksgiving" (Psalm 28:7). There's many ways to praise:

Praising can be in the form of singing: "I will sing to the LORD as long as I live. I will praise my God to my last breath!" (Psalm 104:33); "Sing to God, you kingdoms of the earth. Sing praises to the Lord" (Psalm 68:32); "I will sing of your love and justice, LORD. I will praise you with songs" (Psalm 101:1).

Praising can be reflected in prayer: "I will call upon the LORD, who is worthy to be praised; So shall I be saved from my enemies" (2 Samuel 22:4 NKJV); "Accept my prayer like a gift of burning incense, the words I lift up like an evening sacrifice" (Psalm 141:2 ERV); "Rejoice always, pray continually, give thanks in all circumstances, for this is God's will for you in Christ Jesus" (1 Thessalonians 5:16-18 NIV).

Sharing with others the goodness of God is a form of praise: "My tongue will proclaim your righteousness, your praises all day long" (Psalm 35:28 NIV); "Give thanks to the Lord and call out to him! Tell the nations what he has done!" (1 Chronicles 16:8 ERV); "I will proclaim your name to my brothers and sisters. I will praise you among your assembled people" (Psalm 22:22-23).

And thanking Him throughout the day for all He has done and continues to do in your life is praise: "O our God, we thank you and praise your glorious name!" (1 Chronicles 29:13); "It is good to give thanks to the LORD, to sing praises to the Most High" (Psalm 92:1); "He alone is your God, the only one who is worthy of your praise, the one who has done these mighty miracles that you have seen with your own eyes" (Deuteronomy 10:21).

I praise the Lord always for blessing Samantha's life. For taking that tiny baby with a mass bulging out of her head and wires crossing her body, and enabling her to graduate with honors from college with an associate of arts degree at the age of eighteen, a few weeks before she even graduated high school! For allowing her to defy medical odds by graduating a few years later from the University of Central Florida with a bachelor's degree. For His healing hand on her when she had her only shunt revision at the age of eight and two random seizures during college—the only other medical issues related to the problems from her birth. The seizures are being controlled by medication and Samantha is healthy and extremely bright. Praise the Lord, she is doing miraculously well!

I also give thanks to the Lord for my other two children. Even though I was told my chances of having another child with a birth defect doubled with each one, Kaci and Jacob were born completely healthy and are leading happy, productive lives. This is by the grace and mercy of our Lord—praise God!

Praise is lifting up the name of Jesus while humbling ourselves. It is declaring: "You are my Lord. Every good thing I have comes from you" (Psalm 16:2 ERV). It is giving adoration to our Father: "For everything comes from him and exists by his power and is intended for his glory" (Romans 11:36).

There are countless reasons to give God thanks and we should always remember to be like the one thankful leper and not the other nine, as told in Luke 17:11-19:

> As Jesus continued on toward Jerusalem, he reached the border between Galilee and Samaria. As he entered a village there, ten men with leprosy stood at a distance, crying out, "Jesus, Master, have mercy on us!"
>
> He looked at them and said, "Go show yourselves to the priests." And as they went, they were cleansed of their leprosy.
>
> One of them, when he saw that he was healed, came back to Jesus, shouting, "Praise God!" He fell

> to the ground at Jesus' feet, thanking him for what he had done. This man was a Samaritan.
>
> Jesus asked, "Didn't I heal ten men? Where are the other nine? Has no one returned to give glory to God except this foreigner?" And Jesus said to the man, "Stand up and go. Your faith has healed you."

It's easy to praise when things are going well. But what about the times when you don't have the strength to lift your hands or even your eyes? Your voice is hoarse from tears and there's no dance left in your step? You can begin to praise by remembering all the goodness of God. Praise isn't a feeling but a choice. Praise doesn't come from understanding our circumstances—it comes by understanding who God is. The Lord is still worthy to be praised no matter how you feel.

Many of the Psalms start out with David lamenting his situation, but end in praise. When you aren't in a praiseworthy mood, begin to think about all that the Lord has already done for you and what He still promises to do, and soon you'll feel a praise coming on. Sometimes you have to activate your praise by faith and then trust God will match your spirit, heart and mind to that praise.

When problems are near, that's often when the Lord seems the most distant. Praise keeps you from being pulled away from God by the things of this world. It draws you into a deeper relationship with Him. The Lord made us to glorify Him and He inhabits the praises of His people. Psalm 89:15 says: "Happy are those who hear the joyful call to worship, for they will walk in the light of your presence, Lord."

After King Solomon brought the Ark back to the newly constructed Temple, those in attendance praised the Lord and then experienced His presence in a mighty way.

Dressed in fine linen robes, the Levites played cymbals, lyres, and harps. One hundred and twenty trumpet playing priests joined them, along with singers. Together they all praised and worshipped the Lord, giving thanks to Him. *"At that moment a thick cloud filled the Temple of the Lord. The priests could not continue their service because of the cloud, for the glorious presence of the Lord filled the Temple of God"* (2 Chronicles 5:13-14 emphasis added).

Look beyond the natural. Let praise be your lifeline of hope. Proclaim like the psalmist: "As for me, I will always have hope; I will praise you more and more. My mouth will tell of your righteous deeds, of your saving acts all day long—though I know not how to relate them all" (Psalm 71:14-15 NIV).

Even when you don't feel joyful, act like it and watch your attitude change. When you start praising God for the things He's already done, your attitude of gratitude will give you hope for the things to come.

"Why am I discouraged? Why is my heart so sad? I will put my hope in God! I will praise him again—my Savior and my God!" (Psalm 42:5-7).

Just like the nightingale, sing beautifully in the darkest of nights. An act of diminishment comes into play when you place God in front of your problems. Troubles become smaller in the shadow of the Almighty. So does the devil.

Satan hates praise. He wants to keep you depressed, but praise brings joy. While his goal is to keep you in bondage, praise sets you free and silences the devil. Psalm 8:2 says: "Through the praise of children and infants you have established a stronghold against your enemies, to silence the foe and the avenger" (NIV).

There is great power in genuine praise. John 4:23 tells us: "But the time is coming—indeed it's here now—when true worshipers will worship the Father in spirit and in truth. The Father is looking for those who will worship him that way."

The Lord knows when people are simply going through the motions: "These people honor me with their lips, but their hearts are far from me" (Matthew 15:8). The Lord is not referencing those of us who at times might need an extra boost to get into the spirit of praising, but He's warning those who continually go through the motions and operate in fake praise.

Truly praising when everything is going wrong confuses the devil—and gives us great victories! Chains are released (like when Paul and Silas sang and praised the Lord even though they had been beaten and jailed). Walls come tumbling down (like the walls of Jericho after shouts of praise).

Enemies are defeated, like the army of "ites" who marched against Jehoshaphat and the people of Judah. Even though the people of Judah were terrified, they sought the Lord and praised Him through prayer. And the Lord answered:

> ...Do not be afraid! Don't be discouraged by this mighty army, for the battle is not yours, but God's. Tomorrow, march out against them. ... But you will not even need to fight. Take your positions; then stand still and watch the LORD's victory. He is with you, O people of Judah and Jerusalem. Do not be afraid or discouraged. Go out against them tomorrow, for the LORD is with you!" (2 Chron. 20:15-17)

Then King Jehoshaphat and all the people of Judah and Jerusalem worshiped the Lord. Singers were appointed to walk ahead of the army and praise the Lord all along the way. "At the very moment they began to sing and give praise, the Lord caused the armies of Ammon, Moab, and Mount Sier to start fighting among themselves....Not one single one of the enemy had escaped" (22-24).

God works miraculously through praise, and we are overcomers! Giving glory to the Lord reminds us of His greatness, which gives us strength and a new perspective. He is the King of Kings and Lord of All, the Alpha and Omega, the Beginning and the End, our Redeemer, Comforter, Provider, Prince of Peace, Savior, Deliverer, Healer, the One who loves us with an everlasting love.

Joyful thoughts can't help but bring a joyful heart. Begin to praise and draw closer to God. Watch the enemy retreat, thanksgiving replace negativity, your spirits rise, and fresh hope overshadow your circumstances. Go ahead, make some music and dance in the rain!

PRAYER

Lord, You are worthy to be praised. I want to live my life with an attitude of praise, always remembering all that You've already done for me, all that You promise to do, and all that You are. Help me to dance in the rain and sing in the darkest of nights even when I don't feel like it, because there is power in praise and there is victory. Give me a joyful heart to always worship in spirit and in truth. Through my sincere praise, break every chain and set me free! In the name of Jesus, the Mighty One, I pray, Amen!

CHAPTER 19

RAINBOWS
Promises of God

I have set my rainbow in the clouds, and it will be the sign of the covenant between me and the earth (Genesis 9:13).

As the last drop of water hits the ground and mist from the storm dissipates, rays of sunshine pierce through the clouds and illuminate arched bands of vivid colors. While popular leprechaun folklore may entice you to search for the end of the rainbow and a pot of gold, don't bother because you will never find them.

The promises of God, however, are easy to find. Scripture assures us: "And if you search for him with all your heart and soul, you will find him" (Deuteronomy 4:29).

We've all endured broken promises and we've all broken promises, but God never breaks His promises. Psalm 89:34 confirms: "I won't break my agreement or go back on my word" (CEV).

The Bible declares God cannot lie. Numbers 23:19 says: "God is not a man; he will not lie. God is not a human being; his decisions will not change. If he says he will do something, then he will do it. If he makes a promise, then he will do what he promised."

The Bible says, "Then they will have the hope of eternal life that God promised long ago. And God never tells a lie!" (Titus 1:2 CEV). Hebrews 6:18 also assures us: "So God has given both his promise and his oath. These two things are unchangeable because it is impossible for God to lie. Therefore, we who have fled to him for refuge can have great confidence as we hold to the hope that lies before us."

We can trust everything God's Word says, and His Word will equip us to handle every challenge in our lives. Life-changing power is available through His Word. The Lord promises: "As the rain and the snow come down from the heaven, and do not return to it without watering the earth and making it bud and flourish, so that it yields seed for the sower and bread for the eater, *so is my word that goes out from My mouth. It will not return to me empty, but will accomplish what I desire and achieve the purpose for which I sent it*" (Isaiah 55:10-11 NIV, emphasis added).

Praise the Lord who can bless misfortunes and give us beauty for ashes!

My little girl is now an adult and living in Japan where she was a missionary for three years and shared the gospel through teaching English classes. She is now working as a teacher at a Japanese Junior High School and aspires to make Japan her lifelong home. We believe she is right where God wants her, at least for this season. Interestingly, at the age of eight Samantha became obsessed with anything having to do with Japan. She wrote reports for school about Japan, dressed in kimonos, ate Japanese food, enjoyed anime, and even chose her university because they offered Japanese language classes. She felt in her heart God was calling her to Japan and she is living proof that the Lord does have a plan and a purpose for each of us if we are open to it, and He really is in control.

I felt His promise to me on that cold tile floor and I've seen it fulfilled. What started out as a warning to "just love her," turned into Samantha excelling at academics, living in a foreign country on her own, and being used mightily by the Lord for His Kingdom. When we lay all our own expectations down, He creates something even more glorifying than we could ever have imagined.

The Lord blessed us with a miracle, but if He had chosen the doctor's outlook for Samantha's life instead of gifting her in the ways He did, she'd still bring the greatest joy to my life. God's purpose is always best and He will give us what we need for His plan.

God can work just as mightily in your life! He is as faithful to you as He was to Abraham, Noah, Jacob, Moses, Joseph, Job, David, Hannah, Rahab, and so many others. The Bible is filled with the promises of God and 2 Corinthians 1:20 says: "For no matter how many promises God has made, they are "Yes" in Christ. And so through him the "Amen" is spoken by us to the glory of God" (NIV).

When we search for the promises of God more precious than any pot of gold, it's essential to recognize that God's promises are not earthbound blessings but heaven bound missions. We may long to take His Word as a guarantee for prosperity and everything good in our lives, but the Lord's purposes are Kingdom-minded. The people of Israel desired Jesus to be an earthly king and deliver them from their Roman oppressors, and likewise, we often view His promises from our perspective and wishful thinking rather than the goal of glorifying Him.

God operates on His own timetable, but rest assured, His promises will come to pass. He does exactly what He says He will do—just not always at the time we think He should. The Lord sees beginning to end and we don't. "Let us hold tightly without wavering to the hope we affirm, for God can be trusted to keep his promise" (Hebrews 10:23).

God's promises are either unconditional or conditional, and can be in the form of a blessing or a warning. The unconditional promises of God do not require us to do anything to receive them. They are "no strings attached" guarantees. He made an unconditional promise during Noah's time when He placed a rainbow in the sky after destroying everything on earth except the inhabitants of the Ark:

> The rainbow that I have put in the sky will be my sign to you and to every living creature on earth. It will remind you that I will keep this promise forever. When I send clouds over the earth, and a rainbow appears in the sky, I will remember my promise to you and to all other living creatures. Never again will I let floodwaters destroy all life. When I see the rainbow in the sky, I will always remember the promise that I have made to every living creature. The rainbow will be the sign of that solemn promise. (Genesis 9:12-17 CEV)

Here are a few more examples of unconditional truths that are reflections of the Lord's glorious second coming:

"Jesus has been taken from you into heaven, but someday he will return from heaven in the same way you saw him go!" (Acts 1:9-11).

"Indeed the time is coming when all the dead in their graves will hear the voice of God's Son, and they will rise again. Those who have done good will rise to experience eternal life, and those who have continued in evil will rise to experience judgment" (John 5:28-29).

We don't have to do anything to receive these unconditional promises. The events will happen regardless. Conditional promises, on the other hand, are tied to a requirement. The blessings follow action on our part. God's conditions, though, are never out of our reach and are always used to build our character, draw us into a closer relationship with Him, and to make us more like Jesus.

Sometimes you can spot a conditional promise by the use of the word "if." Others reflect a cause and effect attached to the blessing. There are literally thousands of promises listed in the Bible, so here are just a few conditional examples (emphasis added):

"But from there you will search again for the Lord your God, *and if you search for him with all your heart and soul*, you will find him" (Deuteronomy 4:29).

Therefore, *if anyone is in Christ*, the new creation has come; The old has gone, the new is here! (2 Corinthians 5:17 NIV).

But seek first his kingdom and his righteousness, and all these things will be given to you as well (Matthew 6:33 NIV).

"And we know that God causes everything to work together for the good of *those who love God* and are called according to his purpose for them" (Romans 8:28).

"Then Jesus said, '*Come to me*, all of you who are weary and carry heavy burdens, and I will give you rest. *Take my yoke upon you.* Let me teach you, because I am humble and gentle at heart, and you will find rest for your souls. For my yoke is easy to bear, and the burden I give you is light'" (Matthew 11:28-30).

"*If any of you lack wisdom, you should ask God*, who gives generously to all without finding fault, and it will be given to you" (James 1:5 NIV).

"*But those who hope in the* LORD *will renew their strength. They will soar on wings like eagles; they will run and not grow weary, they will walk and not be faint*" (Isaiah 40:31 NIV).

"The LORD will fight for you; *you need only to be still*" (Exodus 14:14 NIV).

"*Trust in the* LORD *with all your heart; do not depend on your own understanding. Seek his will in all you do*, and he will show you which path to take" (Proverbs 3:5-6).

Notice all of these glorious assurances involve putting God first. Each of us bears a responsibility to the relationship. God's part is already guaranteed, so you can boldly assert God's promises *as long as you do your part*. These vows are yours to claim by making Jesus the Lord of your life and following His provisions.

God's conditional promises teach us obedience and trust, and in turn, bless us. Since "every good gift and every perfect gift is from above,"[1] your blessings may not always be exactly in the form you want, but the Lord in His infinite wisdom will provide the good and perfect blessings you need in order to fulfill His purpose for you.

Believing in the promises of God will help you weather the storms. The Bible is full of promises for every challenge in life. Whether you are being ravaged by wildfires of anger, tossed around by cyclones of unforgiveness, or battered by waves of grief, pick up your Bible and be encouraged by the uplifting promises of God.

Probably the most familiar and beloved promise is found in John 3:16, which guarantees that no matter what happens to us in this life, we have eternity with Christ to look forward to when we believe. "Yes, God loved the world so much that he gave his only Son, *so that everyone who believes in him would not be lost but have eternal life*" (emphasis added).

Rainbows

Remember, this world is not our home. The Lord promises even greater things to come. There will be a new heaven and a new earth and we will live together with God:

> ..."Look, God's home is now among his people! He will live with them, and they will be his people. God himself will be with them. He will wipe every tear from their eyes, and there will be no more death or sorrow or crying or pain. All these things are gone forever."
>
> And the one sitting on the throne said, "Look, I am making everything new!" And then he said to me, "Write this down, for what I tell you is trustworthy and true." And he also said, "It is finished! I am the Alpha and the Omega—the Beginning and the End. To all who are thirsty I will give freely from the springs of the water of life. All who are victorious will inherit all these blessings, and I will be their God, and they will be my children. (Revelations 21:3-7)

Until that time, enjoy peace in the promise that you are a beloved child of God. He loves you unconditionally. Even when you don't deserve it, He still loves you. When you are weak, when you've sinned, when you are selfish, when you ignore Him…He still loves you. His love is not based on your actions. Because He is God, His love doesn't change whether you are good or bad—His steadfast love remains the same. He doesn't love you because of who you are but because of who He is, and God is love (1 John 4:8). Rejoice in the promise that He loves you with an everlasting love!

"'For the mountains may move and the hills disappear, but even then my faithful love for you will remain. My covenant of blessing will never be broken,' says the LORD, who has mercy on you" (Isaiah 54:10).

By holding tightly to the covenant of His faithful love and standing under the covering of all the other promises of God, you can endure any of life's storms. The Lord promises: "And be sure of this: I am with you always, even to the end of the age" (Matthew 28:20).

PRAYER

Lord Jesus, I am standing on the promises of God and I thank You for the assurance of eternal life with You when I believe. Thank You also for the countless other blessings You've given me and for those still to come. I am holding tight to Your promises and Your unconditional love, and I'm believing I can weather any storm as long as I am with You. Your Word is more precious to me than gold. When the storms are fierce, please help me to remember there's a rainbow on the other side of the clouds. In the name of Jesus, My Umbrella in the Storm, I pray, Amen!

INVITATION

Accepting the Free Gift of the Umbrella

Since life is full of storms, I hope you packed your Umbrella for the journey. Even though an unexpected rainstorm can sometimes catch you off-guard without the protection of one, you can always have the safety of Jesus when the storms of life hit. This Umbrella can be yours for free—the shelter of Christ is a gift.

To receive this Umbrella, you must "believe in the Lord Jesus and you will be saved" (Acts 16:30-31 NIV). Have faith in Jesus as the Son of God who came to earth and lived a sinless life so He could die on the cross as the penalty for your sins, but is now alive and interceding on your behalf. 1 Timothy 2:5 says: "For there is one God and one mediator between God and men, the man Christ Jesus."

Believe John 3:16 which declares: "Yes, God loved the world so much that he gave his only Son, so that everyone who believes in him would not be lost but have eternal life."

Trust Jesus Christ loves you with an everlasting love and wants you to spend eternity with Him!

Accept the truth of John 14:6: "I am the way, the truth, and the life. No one comes to the Father except through Me."

Understand you are a sinner in need of a Savior and without the sacrifice of Jesus you could never be in the presence of holy God.

When you have put your trust in Jesus and are ready to accept this life-saving Umbrella, Romans 10:9-10 says: "If you declare with your mouth, 'Jesus is Lord,' and believe in your heart that God raised him from the dead, you will be saved. For it is with your heart that you believe and are justified, and it is with your mouth that you profess your faith and are saved."

You can pray any words spoken from your heart (there is no specific formula), but here is a sample prayer:

> Heavenly Father, please forgive me. I admit I am a sinner in need of a Savior and I thank You for sending Your one and only Son to die for my sins so I could be set free and have eternal life. I believe in my heart that Jesus rose from the dead, and I ask You, Jesus, to become Lord of my life and to help me live in a way that is pleasing to You. Thank You, Lord, for the precious gift of salvation and for Your eternal love and protection. In Jesus' name I pray, Amen!

If you've prayed with true conviction and belief, Romans 10:13 affirms: "Whoever calls on the name of the Lord shall be saved."

Congratulations, you are a part of God's family and can confidently hold onto the Umbrella as protection through all storms!

DISCUSSION QUESTIONS

CHAPTER 1: UNEXPECTED STORMS
- Share a time when you were hit by an unexpected storm.
- Did you ever notice warning signs of an impending storm? What were they?
- Why should we not panic in a storm?
- What should we do instead?
- Was there ever a time when you felt the Lord was "sleeping on the job" or ignoring you?
- What brought you into a closer relationship with Him?
- What do you struggle with most in trusting God?
- Paul was convinced he was following God's calling by persecuting Christians. What are some examples of other people who zealously tackled a wrong cause?
- Share your views about the statement: "I find more assurance in serving an Almighty God who can fix anything if He chooses, rather than relying on a God who can't change something even if He wanted to."

CHAPTER 2: DOPPLER RADAR
- Do you have any interesting ways to predict weather?
- List other scriptures that inform us we will face trials.
- Name some tactics satan uses to prey on people.
- Discuss specific ways satan attempts to attack you.

- Share a time when the storm actually caused some much needed rain.
- What helps you to look beyond the rain clouds?

CHAPTER 3: BATTEN DOWN THE HATCHES
- What things have you done to prepare for natural disasters?
- How do you feel we should prepare spiritually for trials?
- How can we seek shelter in the Lord?
- What is a good spiritual evacuation plan?
- Which piece of armor is most assuring to you?
- Which piece of armor is hardest for you to put on?

CHAPTER 4: CYCLONES
- Discuss whether you have ever needed to forgive someone or if someone has ever needed to forgive you.
- Have you ever forgiven but struggled with forgetting?
- Could you have forgiven like Joseph did? If not, what would keep you from forgiving?
- Have you ever had unforgiveness eat away at your health?
- Have you ever wanted to exact revenge but pulled back and left it to the Lord instead? If so, has God resolved it yet, and if not, do you have peace it's in His hands and can you move on?
- Are there any situations you wish you would have left to the Lord to avenge? Is there still a chance to rectify the matter, and if so, how can you handle it in a godly manner?
- Discuss people like Corrie ten Boom who have forgiven others when it almost seems humanly impossible to do so. Could you do the same if faced with such atrocious situations?
- Do you need to forgive yourself for something? What can you do to set yourself free?

Discussion Questions

CHAPTER 5: TSUNAMIS

- What forms of grief have you experienced?
- Were there people to help you through the grief who understood your pain?
- What trials have you suffered through that now give you the compassion and experience to be used by God to help others?
- Is there a particular scripture that's helped you when grieving?
- Share your thoughts about the fact: "Jesus cried."
- Does your grief differ between the death of a Christian and the death of someone who is a nonbeliever?
- How can you use that difference to motivate yourself and others to share the Good News?
- If you were to rename yourself to match your circumstances, what name would you have given yourself during a time of grief?

CHAPTER 6: TORNADOES

- Have you ever experienced an actual tornado?
- Do you sometimes struggle with envy or jealousy?
- What tends to be triggers for you?
- Share a time you were especially envious.
- Have you ever had a relationship ruined because of jealousy, either on your part or someone else's?
- Have you experienced envy in the workplace?
- How about in ministry?
- Discuss God being a jealous God.
- Do you feel there are times when jealousy is good? If so, why?
- Share your feelings about social media.
- Has social medial ever caused a twister in you?
- What are some ways to overcome "the green-eyed monster?"

CHAPTER 7: OVERCAST
- If not too personal, share health issues you or someone you know has battled.
- Have well-meaning people ever tried to say you could be healed if you just had enough faith?
- Have you ever shared that same reasoning with others?
- Do you ever feel illness is a punishment for sin?
- What are your thoughts on prayers for healing that were not answered in the way you wanted them to be answered?
- Have you ever recognized a higher purpose to incidents of suffering?

CHAPTER 8: WILDFIRES
- Have you or someone you know struggled with anger?
- Do you feel anger is ever justified, and if so, when?
- Are you surprised about the times when God got angry?
- What are some ways you quench the fires of anger?
- Share instances when you've been burned by anger.
- Have you ever been angry at God?
- Do you think it's ever okay to be mad at the Lord?
- How should people handle their anger towards God?

CHAPTER 9: TROPICAL DEPRESSION
- Do little things ever steal your joy?
- What is the difference between happiness and joy?
- Are there times when you find yourself worrying instead of trusting?
- How can you turn worry into trust?
- Share some of the blessings in your life.
- What are some things you can do to become more joyful?

Discussion Questions

CHAPTER 10: INNER AND OUTER RAINBANDS
- What does the word "sin" mean?
- Can you accept the Lord's correction when you've messed up?
- When you've sinned are you quick to ask for forgiveness?
- Have you ever carried the guilt of your sins long after God has already forgiven you? What can you do to move beyond that?
- Have you ever had to punish your children when you really didn't want to but knew they needed to learn from their mistakes?
- Did it change your love for them?
- The story of Hosea and Gomer is such a beautiful expression of God's enduring love for us. Share other scriptures/stories that reminds you of God's unconditional love.

CHAPTER 11: STORM SHELTER
- Do you tend to draw closer to God in the sunshine or in the pouring rain?
- What can we do to stay close to God even in the good times?
- How can we keep ourselves from becoming distant with God during tough times?
- Think of trials you've gone through that have actually increased your faith.
- Reflect on challenges that have tested your faith.
- Have you ever experienced hardships you later were thankful for?
- Are there instances where you are now grateful the Lord didn't answer your prayers the way you originally wanted Him to?
- What are some things we can do to get back to our First Love?

CHAPTER 12: RIDING THE STORM OUT
- Does prayer tend to be your last resort or your first?

- Do you find it easy or difficult to have an intimate relationship with the Lord?
- How does unconfessed sin keep us distant from God?
- Have you ever had relationships (children, spouse, family, friends) suffer because you didn't spend enough quality time together?
- Have you ever felt disconnected from God?
- Did you learn anything from a time when God seemed distant?
- What can you do to spend more time with God?
- Do your prayers tend to be "arrow prayers" or more detailed?
- Do you feel short prayers are just as powerful as long prayers? Why or why not?
- Discuss things you can start doing to have a closer relationship with the Lord.

CHAPTER 13: TRAVEL ALERT

- Share times when you felt confident in what you were doing, only to then run into challenges.
- Did you turn back or keep going?
- How can we make ourselves like clay in the Potter's hand?
- What are some ways to stay encouraged when storms want to derail our plans?

CHAPTER 14: IN THE EYE OF THE STORM

- Why is it so hard to wait on God?
- What do you find the most difficult during seasons of waiting?
- Do you catch yourself trying to "help" God?
- Is there something you've been waiting for?
- Discuss ways to stand strong during seasons of waiting when satan tries to discourage us.

Discussion Questions

- Have you ever taken matters into your own hands, and if so, how did that turn out?
- How can we "be still" yet keep move forward?
- Do you feel there's a time limit to waiting?
- What does waiting develop?

CHAPTER 15: BLIZZARDS

- Is your personality more action-oriented or wait and see?
- Discuss why God sometimes waits for us to take action before He gives us the blessing.
- Have you experienced Gideon moments when you hid in fear because you didn't feel worthy enough to step out?
- Have you ever been called to move in a way that didn't make sense to you at the time?
- How did God work in that instance?
- What are some ways to move past fear and indecisiveness and into action and faith?

CHAPTER 16: SEA OF STORMS

- What is faith?
- Discuss the Scripture: "For we walk by faith, not by sight" (2 Corinthians 5:7 NKJV).
- How easy is it for you to live by that passage?
- Share times when you've had to operate in blind faith.
- Do you tend to see giants or a land flowing with milk and honey?
- Share ways to stay anchored to Christ.

CHAPTER 17: FLOOD OF GRACE

- Discuss the differences between mercy and grace.

- Have you ever been given a gift you didn't deserve?
- Share a time when God gave you unmerited favor and tell how you felt.
- Explain "but God."
- Share any "but God" moments in your life.

CHAPTER 18: DANCING IN THE RAIN

- Give examples of praise.
- Discuss the power of praise.
- Why do people struggle to praise God during a crisis?
- Why do people forget to praise Him during good times?
- Have you ever praised the Lord when you didn't feel like it, to then find your situation shifting favorably?
- Do your problems ever get in front of God?
- How does praising God during tough times confuse the devil and how can we use that to our advantage?
- What can you do to be able to dance in the rain?

CHAPTER 19: RAINBOWS

- Discuss times when people have broken their word to you.
- How did you react?
- Have you had issues trusting because of broken promises?
- Does that lead you to struggle with believing God will keep His word?
- Why is it often difficult to trust in His timetable?
- What is the difference between conditional and unconditional promises?
- Why is it so important to believe in the promises of God?
- How can we learn to fully rely on the Lord's Word?
- Share some of your favorite promises of God.

Photos

Samantha's First Years

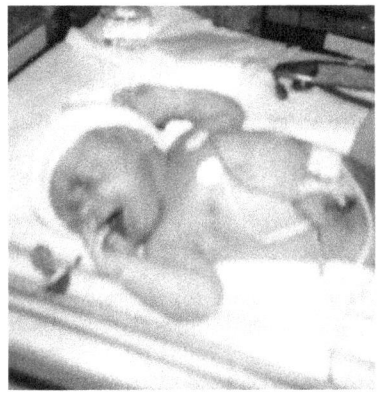
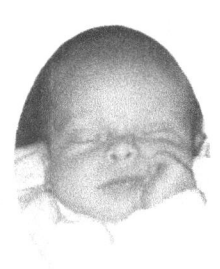

The bulge behind Samantha's ear is her shunt.

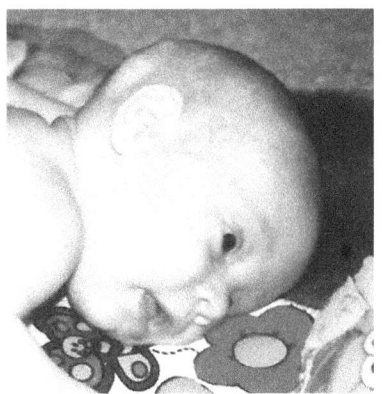

A few of Samantha's many bonnets!

> "We saw a lot of people with bags. We just felt we needed to bless them with something."
>
> **SAMANTHA SHONER, 13,** co-founder of Backpacks 'n Blessings

HELP FOR THE HOMELESS

Flagler family giving out backpacks

By KENYA WOODARD
STAFF WRITER

Barbara Shoner, right, and her children, Samantha, middle, and Jacob, put into backpacks and then distributed to the homeless and to shelters at their home last week. The Shoners began "Backpacks 'n Blessings" — a nonprofit organization to fill and hand out the backpacks in Flagler and Volusia counties.

News-Tribune/KENYA WOODARD

BUNNELL — A trio of children want to make a big difference in the effort to help those without homes.

The Shoner children — Samantha, 13; Kaci, 10; and Jacob, 8 — are the founders of Backpacks 'n Blessings, a nonprofit organization soliciting donations to distribute backpacks to homeless residents of Volusia and Flagler counties.

According to Samantha, the idea first came to her when she saw a homeless man struggling to carry his belongings in a plastic bag. Shortly after, the children began seeing other homeless people in similar situations, she said.

"We saw a lot of people with bags," she said. "We just felt we needed to bless them with something."

The children, who are home-schooled, patterned their organization after a similar nonprofit group that collects suitcases for foster children, mother Barbara Shoner said.

The backpacks are filled with basic items that others may take for granted, such as blankets, socks, ponchos, shampoo, razors, soap, healthy snacks and Bibles. Backpacks for children include a teddy bear.

The Shoners hope to have more than 100 backpacks ready in time for a Dec. 4 Christmas party for homeless people at City Island in Daytona Beach, and to distribute in shelters, Barbara Shoner said.

Though the organization started in the family's living room, the Shoners are promoting their idea using tools inspired by larger, more professional charities.

They produced a DVD slide show for schools, churches and other groups. Their presentations, along with word-of-mouth marketing, so far have yielded 15 backpacks and $1,200, Barbara Shoner said.

Barbara Shoner, a real estate agent and former foster mother, said her children have always wanted to help others. In addition to their backpack mission, the children have adopted a Nicaraguan girl, Nina, to whom they write every week and send packages at Christmas.

The children also regularly visit with seniors at nursing homes, she said.

"They really appreciate what they have because they've seen others who don't have as much as they do," she said.

Randy Croy, executive director of Serenity House in Daytona Beach, applauded the venture.

"What we consider to be small things for us are big to the homeless," said Croy, whose organization serves the area's homeless population. "I think the actual gifts themselves are a blessing."

Part of the Shoners' mission involves teaching others about the causes of homelessness.

"They're just people that have bad situations in their lives and they need help," Samantha Shoner said.

People who are more fortunate shouldn't look down on homeless people, Kaci Shoner said.

"I think people should spend a night homeless so they can see what it's like," she said. "Sometimes it's really cold outside and they have nowhere to go."

kenya.woodard@news-jrnl.com

Volunteer Spotlight | *The Shoner Family*

Barbara and Jacob Shoner, 10, of Bunnell organize backpacks to be given away to the homeless at the Volusia/Flagler County Coalition for the Homeless Center in Daytona Beach on Dec. 13.

SARA A. FAJARDO/ORLANDO SENTINEL

Children recognize need, collect backpacks

By TERRY O. ROEN
SENTINEL STAFF WRITER

DAYTONA BEACH — A homeless man seeking shelter under a bridge from the rain prompted the three Shoner children to create a nonprofit group called Backpacks 'n Blessings to ease the struggles of those less fortunate.

Samantha Shoner, 12, said the family were driving to Calvary Christian Center in Ormond Beach last year from their home in Bunnell when she spotted the man carrying his belongings in "a bunch of plastic bags."

"A lot of people have bad situations in their lives that create hard times for themselves and their families," said Samantha, who is homeschooled along with her siblings, Kaci, 10, and Jacob, 8.

"It feels good to be able to help them and see the look on their faces."

The children have put together and distributed more than 600 backpacks filled with tarps, rain ponchos, toiletries, blankets and Bibles. Some have teddy bears tucked inside for children.

They are planning to ally with homeless shelters throughout the country to take their idea nationwide and distribute the backpacks year round, said their mother, Barbara Shoner, an agent with Infinity Real Estate in Palm Coast.

Families in California, Kentucky, Texas, Tennessee and Ohio have contacted the Shoners to start chapters of Backpacks 'n Blessings.

The Shoners distributed more than 100 backpacks to the homeless at a Christmas party Dec. 4 at City Island in Daytona Beach.

They also gave another 100 to the Volusia Flagler County Coalition for the Homeless in Daytona Beach when they joined with nurses from Halifax Medical Center who collected 260 backpacks and delivered them Dec. 13 on a sleigh ride with Santa.

They are putting together another 200 to distribute after the holidays.

Ted Kuzma, program manager at the coalition, described the Shoner family's contribution as "unique" since they have taken on this mission as a family project.

"Everything they own in life is what they carry," Kuzma said. "When you live on the street you get rained on, and backpacks are impervious to water and help them keep their clothing dry."

Barbara Shoner, 44, said she has been surprised by her children's initiative and drive in distributing the backpacks.

She said they are learning about the business side of charitable organizations by budgeting donations and asking local businesses to contribute to the program.

"My children have always been very compassionate," she said. "They have learned that one person can touch the life of another."

The kids began performing skits and songs at nursing homes six years ago with a program they named "A Joyful Noise."

The Red Hat Club at Indigo Manor, an Ormond Beach facility where they have performed, collected $300 recently to donate to Backpacks 'n Blessings.

The family also has participated in church mission trips to Nicaragua and Honduras.

Backpacks 'n Blessings needs donations of new or gently used backpacks, rain ponchos, lightweight blankets, toiletries, socks, sweatshirts, teddy bears and Bibles.

Nursing Home Ministry

Giving out Backpacks

Governor Rick Scott at High School Graduation

UCF B.A. Graduation

Samantha in Japan

Photos

Natalie Grant Make it Matter Concert

Samantha and Natalie Grant

The author with
Samantha & Natalie Grant

Samantha and Chris Sligh

Umbrella in the Storm

To watch the Channel 6 and Channel 13 news interviews with Samantha about our backpack program, please visit:
www.barbarashoner.com/videochan6.htm
www.barbarashoner.com/videochan13.htm

REVIEW

I sincerely hope you enjoyed reading this book and that it has given you valuable insight into weathering the storms in your life. Please take a moment to share your thoughts. Reviews are valuable to both authors and readers, and even a word or two from you can make a big difference.

Thanks, and may God's love and favor always be upon you.

Review on Amazon
https://www.amazon.com/dp/B07HK21QLS

I want to hear from you. Feel free to contact me with any comments, praise reports or prayer requests:

barbara@barbarashoner.com

or visit my website:
www.barbarashoner.com

ABOUT THE AUTHOR

Barbara Shoner is a learning junkie with a slew of degrees (mostly because five hours is a good night's sleep for her): master's degree in theology, bachelor's degree in biblical studies, paralegal associate degree, certification with the American Association of Christian Counselors, certified TESOL teacher, Realtor, certified travel agent, and a graduate of the school of hard knocks. She's been through countless life storms but continues to hang onto her Umbrella in optimistic Mary Poppins fashion.

Her writing talents blossomed in the fourth grade when she won the Young Authors award for her inspiring book *How the Giraffe Got His Long Neck,* but missed accepting the award because her fear of public speaking kept her hidden in the bathroom during the ceremony! Having conquered that phobia, Barbara accepted three awards at the Florida Movie Festival as the screenwriter and producer of the coming-of-age feature film, *Steadfast,* which has also been awarded The Dove Foundation's Faith-Based and Family Friendly Ages 12+ Seals of Approval. In addition, Barbara wrote study guides for both teens and parents that are based on the movie and give biblical insight and practical advice to relevant

About the Author

topics such as bullying. More information can be found at www.steadfastthemovie.com.

Besides the Lord and her family (and writing, of course), her passions are traveling, hiking, and photography—preferably all at the same time. Adventures include snorkeling with sea lions in the Galapagos Islands, hiking glaciers in Alaska, diving with sharks in Hawaii, riding camels in Dubai, and eating fried maple leaves in Japan (about as adventurous in eating as this girl gets).

Don't miss Barbara's upcoming book: *Stop Worrying! God is Already in Your Tomorrows*. To find out when her next book will be available, please visit her website at www.barbarashoner.com where you can sign up to receive updates and also get her FREE ebook: *Praying by the Word: Discovering the Power in God's Promises*.

Website: www.barbarashoner.com/
Facebook: fb.me/authorbarbarashoner
Twitter: twitter.com/barbara_shoner
Instagram: www.instagram.com/barbarashoner/
Upcoming Blogs: www.joyfulglobetrekker.com
                        www.roadinthewilderness.com

Other Works
(Release date December 6, 2018)

Steadfast the Movie DVD and HD Digital Download
Steadfast the Movie Original Soundtrack
Steadfast the Movie Resource Video
Steadfast Teens Study Guide
Steadfast Parents Study Guide
Steadfast Teens Devotional and Prayer Journal
Steadfast Parents Devotional and Prayer Journal

NOTES

CHAPTER 1
[1] 1 Chronicles 29:11-12

CHAPTER 4
[1] Dearen, Jason. "Family's Excruciating Orlando Journey Ends in Forgiveness." AP News, Associated Press, 16 June 2016, apnews.com/5a9efcab09e24356994a74b52173a27c/familys-excruciating-orlando-journey-ends-forgiveness.
[2] Meek, Pauline Palmer. The Hiding Place. Whitman Pub. Co., 1971.

CHAPTER 8
[1] James 1:19

CHAPTER 9
[1] Meek, Pauline Palmer. The Hiding Place. Whitman Pub. Co., 1971.
[2] Psalm 51:12

CHAPTER 11
[1] Psalm 71:8 NKJV
[2] Psalm 86:15 NKJV

Notes

CHAPTER 12

[1] Psalm 27:4

[2] Philippians 1:21

[3] Hebrews 11:6

[4] Psalm 24:3-4

CHAPTER 13

[1] Psalm 37:23-24 CEV

[2] Psalm 119:133 NIV

[3] Hebrews 13:21

CHAPTER 17

[1] Bowerman, Mary. "Texas Mom Dies Saving Her Daughter during Hurricane Harvey Flooding." USA Today, Gannett Satellite Information Network, 30 Aug. 2017, www.usatoday.com/story/news/nation-now/2017/08/30/texas-mom-dies-saving-her-infant-daughter-during-hurricane-harvey-flooding/615436001/.

[2] Buechner, Frederick. Wishful Thinking: a Seeker's ABC. Mowbray, 1994.

[3] Matthew 18:12-14

[4] Luke 15:11-32

[5] Joshua 2

[6] Genesis 37

[7] Corinthians 9:8

[8] 1 Corinthians 15:10 NKJV

May the Lord bless you
and protect you.
May the Lord smile on you
and be gracious to you.
May the Lord show you his favor
and give you his peace.

Number 6:24-26

www.ingramcontent.com/pod-product-compliance
Lightning Source LLC
Chambersburg PA
CBHW061318040426

42444CB00011B/2705